PRAISE FOR *ROMAN POLANSKI: BEHIND THE SCENES OF HIS CLASSIC EARLY FILMS*

"*Roman Polanski: Behind the Scenes of His Classic Early Films* is a fascinating look at Polanski's formative years in Swinging London—a vital chapter in the director's career, long before his reputation would become forever mired in controversy. Jordan Young draws upon both insightful archival material and an impressive series of personal interviews with Polanski's colleagues and collaborators to provide a highly entertaining and revealing account of the making of *Repulsion*, *Dance of the Vampires*, and the neglected masterpiece *Cul-de-Sac*, which brought both the filmmaker and British cinema to the forefront of the thriving international film scene in the 1960s."— **Christopher Weedman**, coeditor, *Adult Themes: British Cinema and the "X" Certificate in the Long 1960s*

"In our era of political and personal polarization, powerful artists are regularly taken down for all-too-human weaknesses. Director Roman Polanski exemplifies the tragedy of flawed genius. In this book, Young's approach to Polanski's work is refreshingly honest and fascinatingly informative in its celebration and critique of the rare brilliance and clay feet of artist and man."—**Grant Hayter-Menzies**, author, *Staging Emily Dickinson: The History and Enduring Influence of William Luce's 'The Belle of Amherst'*

"The bulk of this essential film book concentrates on the 1966 crazed fruit *Cul-de-Sac*. It's a paranoid, schizophrenic exercise in psychopathy 101. The movie . . . perfectly conforms to events both behind the camera, and those being filmed before it. Seriously, folks, you have to read this to believe it. It's one exhilarating, jaw-dropping ride." —**Mel Neuhaus**, author of *Noir Voyager: Film Noir Movie Reviews from Supervistaramacolorscope*

"Jordan Young's detailed study offers multiple entry points into the cascading array of perverse ironies and ironic perversities that make Roman Polanski's legendary *Cul-de-Sac* a tour de force of norm-breaking 1960s cinema. With his vivid history of the film's troubled production and colorful accounts of the remarkable talents who created it, Young makes a powerful case for renewed appreciation of this darkly glowing jewel and the tenacious brilliance of its rebellious young auteur."—**David Sterritt**, editor-in-chief, *Quarterly Review of Film and Video*

DIRECTED BY ROMAN POLANSKI

SONY COLUMBIA

ROMAN POLANSKI

BEHIND THE SCENES OF HIS CLASSIC EARLY FILMS

Jordan R. Young

APPLAUSE
THEATRE & CINEMA BOOKS

Essex, Connecticut

APPLAUSE
THEATRE & CINEMA BOOKS

An imprint of Globe Pequot, the trade division of
The Rowman & Littlefield Publishing Group, Inc.
4501 Forbes Blvd., Ste. 200
Lanham, MD 20706
www.rowman.com

Distributed by NATIONAL BOOK NETWORK

Library of Congress Cataloging-in-Publication Data Available

ISBN 978-1-4930-6792-3 (cloth: alk. paper)
ISBN 978-1-4930-7270-5 (electronic)

♾️™ The paper used in this publication meets the minimum requirements
of American National Standard for Information Sciences—Permanence of
Paper for Printed Library Materials, ANSI/NISO Z39.48-1992

For Philip and Pearl Young

CONTENTS

COURTESY OF BISON ARCHIVES/PARAMOUNT PICTURES

FOREWORD

Jordan Young's book *Roman Polanski: Behind the Scenes of His Classic Early Films* is a new addition to a large body of works devoted to Roman Polanski, which includes his autobiography, biographies, popular books about his films, and scholarly works conducted in many languages. Its novelty lies in approaching Polanski's work and life from the perspective of production studies. Specifically, Young discusses production of Polanski's early English-language films: *Repulsion*, *Cul-de-Sac*, and *Dance of the Vampires*, detailing the struggles of the young director to obtain funding for his projects, assembling cast and crew, shooting, and promoting his works. In this way Young achieves three goals. First, he creates a convincing portrait of the famous director. Second, he provides an insight into a narrower and wider circle of Polanski's collaborators: his producers, scriptwriters, editors, cinematographers, sound editors, and actors, tracing not only their dealings with Polanski but also their previous and subsequent careers. Third, Young offers an excellent examination of the struggles of an up-and-coming director, outlining many possible problems he might encounter and the skills he needs to possess to overcome them and succeed. Hence, it can serve as a useful manual for any wannabe film director, not least because, despite some changes in film production, brought about by developments in filmmaking and communication technologies, the most important principles of filmmaking have not changed, namely that the director is at the center of film creation, taking responsibility for its failure or success.

The portrait of Polanski emerging from pages of *Roman Polanski: Behind the Scenes of His Classic Early Films* is that of a perfectionist, verging on being obsessive about the smallest details. This is not a new portrait, but Young paints it with meticulousness, describing situations when the director's obsessive nature was most visible, such as ensuring that a plane appears over the heads of his characters in *Cul-de-Sac* at the precise moment when it suited the drama or demanding to reduce a specific sequence to just a couple of frames to achieve the right pace of action. At the same time, he demonstrates that Polanski was an instinctive collaborator, looking for the best people for the job and encouraging his cast to improvise dialogue. He was also prepared to change the course of the film when somebody offered a better idea than his own. Polanski's almost religious worship of cinema art and the desire to serve it ultimately resulted in him getting everybody on his side. This worship of cinema Young justly links to Polanski's troubled life, full of pain, misery, and controversy, from which it provided an escape.

Young notes that among Polanski's collaborators, Krzysztof Komeda, who scored most of his films up to the composer's death in 1969, was the closest to the director. This was not so much a matter of speaking the same mother tongue, because Komeda was taciturn, as much as it was understanding the mood of Polanski's films. Admittedly, Polanski's early movies are more about creating a specific mood than exciting action or relatable characters. There is the mood of absurdity and fatalism, with all the macabre humour attached to it. The closeness to Komeda and, in some measure, to the scriptwriter Gérard Brach, might have also something to do with the fact that Polanski did not need to interact with them on the set, where he was understandably stressed and exhausted, but in more relaxed circumstances.

Young devotes most of his attention to *Cul-de-Sac* because he—and many of Polanski's fans—regard it as his greatest achievement, even against the background of such commercial and critical successes as *Rosemary's Baby*, *Chinatown*, and *The Pianist*. This is because of *Cul-de-Sac*'s utter perfectionism and an inability to pinpoint it to any genre or cinematic tradition, resulting in a certain surplus of meaning and mystery. At one point, Young quotes critic David Sterritt, who wrote that "There's no questioning the artistry of the hyperactive, ultrainventive film, which spits out more visual ideas per scene than [almost] any sixties picture." *Cul-de-Sac* affords such a treatment also because of the sheer complications in its production, beginning with securing financing, finding a suitable location, struggling with bad weather and bad food on set, as well as unfriendly, inward-looking locals, actors mimicking the mutual hostility pertaining to their characters, and the imperative to finish the film before the director was ready to leave the set. As for documenting what could go wrong when making the film, *Cul-de-Sac* is a perfect case study. Equally, it provides an excellent analysis of a film maturing with the passing of time, revealing its qualities to new generations of cinema buffs and becoming a cult film, thanks to opportunities afforded by new distribution technologies, such as DVD and Blu-ray.

With his expert knowledge of cinema, especially arthouse films, Young locates *Cul-de-Sac* in the context of European and US cinematic modernism, works of such auteurs as Michelangelo Antonioni, Jean-Luc Godard, and Robert Altman. He demonstrates that in its quirkiness and visual inventiveness it has much in common with them, but also that Polanski, coming from behind the Iron Curtain, found it harder to succeed than these western masters, who worked on their own territory. At the same time, he shows that Polanski is ultimately a cosmopolitan or rather nonnational director, who is governed more by his interest in human nature as such, than specific national traditions and identities, or at least this was the case when he shot his three classic films.

Roman Polanski: Behind the Scenes of His Classic Early Films is a welcome addition to the studies about Polanski because in recent years, interest in the director's private life, especially his sexual encounter with the teenage Samantha Geimer, has eclipsed interest in his films and even led to calls to "cancel" him. Young demonstrates that those who resist such calls will be rewarded with a cinematic feast, while not denying them the right to examine and condemn Polanski's off-screen conduct.

Ewa Mazierska

Ewa Mazierska is the author of Roman Polanski: The Cinema of a Cultural Traveller *and other studies.*

Polanski on the set of Pirates. COURTESY OF BISON ARCHIVES/CANNON

PREFACE

Few filmmakers of any era can lay claim to a résumé burnished by the likes of *The Pianist, Tess, An Officer and a Spy, The Ghost Writer, Oliver Twist, Death and the Maiden*, the blockbuster successes *Chinatown* and *Rosemary's Baby*, and the Oscar-nominated film that started it all, *Knife in the Water*. Roman Polanski has devoted his life to his work at great sacrifice.

As William Faulkner once proclaimed, "The writer's only responsibility is to his art. He will be completely ruthless if he is a good one. . . . Everything goes by the board: honor, pride, decency." For all his crimes and misdemeanors, Polanski's films deserve to be judged on their own merits and not viewed merely through the prism of scandal and controversy.

Roman Polanski: Behind the Scenes of His Classic Early Films is a portrait of the artist in the act of creation. I believe it is the first book of its kind on Polanski, as opposed to the many volumes written without his cooperation by people who never once met or spoke with him.

This off-camera exploration offers a candid look at the Academy Award-winning director during the making of his first three English-language films, *Repulsion, Dance of the Vampires*, and especially *Cul-de-Sac*—the film he has often called his best—conversely a movie made under the worst possible conditions by a crew who hated each other and a cast barely on speaking terms. The reader will hopefully be transported to the set of this offbeat classic, looking over his shoulder and watching him direct.

Cul-de-Sac won the grand prize at a major international film festival before the critics bludgeoned it to death and banished it to the underground film circuit decades ago—only to have it rise from the ashes and find a new legion of passionate admirers today on DVD, Blu-ray, and streaming services. And why not? Few films are as novel the second time around as the first, yet none of this picture's deliciously bizarre quality has dissipated over the years. The film has retained every fiber of its off-the-wall weirdness, its singular blend of kink and quirk as fresh and funny today as when it was first hatched.

It was Samuel Beckett, whose influence hangs over *Cul-de-Sac* like a rain cloud, who led me coincidentally to Polanski, by way of Beckett's devoted interpreter, Jack MacGowran (for whom Polanski wrote *Dance of the Vampires*). I first saw *Cul-de-Sac* on a college film society double bill with *Repulsion* the day before I interviewed MacGowran in 1972, the year before his death. His untimely passing prompted me to write a biography of the actor, for which I interviewed not only Polanski but also Donald Pleasence, Lionel Stander, and producer Gene Gutowski, as well as 100 others.

I met Polanski in his office at Paramount Pictures in Hollywood in 1974, just after he completed editing *Chinatown*. He emanated such warmth and humanity during the hour we spent together I have considered him a friend ever since.

I felt that same warmth the following year in London when Polanski's secretary arranged for me a private screening of his personal print of *Dance of the Vampires*. As I settled in to watch the original European version of *The Fearless Vampire Killers*—in essence the director's cut, then unavailable in the United States—the projectionist kindly brought me a cup of tea. "Friend of Roman's, friend of everyone's," he said with a smile.

The idea for this book hovered for years before making a landing. As *Cul-de-Sac*'s 50th anniversary approached, I felt the time to get started was "now or never," then decided to drop the project unless

Polanski agreed to cooperate by providing access to the shooting script. Happily, he acquiesced and sent me a copy, along with production call sheets and sketches he made. Ironically, Gutowski died in Warsaw the same day I got the green light from Paris.

This expedition is a lot like a detective story. Everyone had their own version of the truth, which seems perfectly in tune with the thread that runs through so many of Polanski's films—from *Chinatown* to *Death and the Maiden* to *An Officer and a Spy*—that frenzied attempt to ferret out the truth.

If everyone I spoke with about *Cul-de-Sac* agreed on all aspects of the film's backstory, this would be a dull book. I welcomed the disparity I came upon as eagerly as any playwright, who knows conflict is a prerequisite of good drama. I have tried, however, to remain unbiased and act as a moderator; Tony Klinger, son of financier Michael Klinger, was disinclined to talk until I assured him I was open to all points of view. The passing of time presented further issues. Even first assistant director Roger Simons had to admit, despite his remarkable memory for details, there were bits and pieces he had forgotten.

This account is not always a flattering one, though I have tried to remain as fair and impartial as possible. My perspective may be colored by my encounter with Polanski, whom I found to be genuinely kind and friendly, bearing little resemblance to the one often depicted in the media. I did not give him approval over the final manuscript.

For his reputation as a demanding individual, Polanski made no demands and set forth no conditions for his cooperation. He declined to answer further questions, however, apparently feeling he'd exhausted the subject, preferring, instead, to devote his energies to new endeavors. As he has said, "the movies have always spoken for themselves."

Jordan R. Young
November 2021

PROLOGUE

"If I had the choice to relive my life, I would not. Under no circumstances,"[1] Roman Polanski once told a correspondent for *People* magazine. "If you could live your life over again, would you really want to?" he implored a writer, when asked to elucidate. "If I balance the good things that have happened to me with the bad, there's been more bad, and the bad has been more painful. . . . I wouldn't live it over again."[2]

Movies provided a joyous escape from the reality of his childhood. Born August 18, 1933, Raymond Polanski—soon calling himself Roman, "Romek" to his friends—found himself addicted from the beginning, entranced by silent comedies, cartoons, and the likes of *Snow White and the Seven Dwarfs*, *The Adventures of Robin Hood*, and later *Citizen Kane*. "It was very unpatriotic to go to see the movies. The slogan was, 'Only pigs go to the movies.' But a lot of people went,"[3] he told a TV interviewer. "Even when the Nazis showed anti-Semitic propaganda films, I'd be glued to the barbed wire,"[4] he commented to another.

The impact films would have on him is immeasurable. One of the key elements in Polanski's films—atmosphere—can be traced back to one of his all-time favorites, Carol Reed's *Odd Man Out* (1947). As he told *Cahiers du Cinema*, "What I like is an extremely realistic setting in which there is something that does not quite fit with the real. That is what gives it atmosphere."[5] As the director elaborated to James Greenberg, "The whole atmosphere strangely resembles my childhood in Krakow." The impact was so great, "I always feel I'm trying to copy *Odd Man Out*."[6]

Laurence Olivier's *Hamlet* (1948) also had a strong influence on him. "I wanted to make the kinds of films where you feel the walls around you,"[7] he asserted. The picture, which he saw some 24 times, launched Polanski on a Shakespearean odyssey, reading the Bard's plays in Polish, and envisioning what they would be like as films. A less lofty, albeit unrealized, ambition, a prank inspired by a scene in the Laurel and Hardy comedy *Swiss Miss*, was to move a friend's mother's grand piano from her drawing room into the street.

"Art and poetry, the land of imagination, always seemed more real to me . . . than the narrow confines of my environment,"[8] Polanski recalled in his memoirs. Though he was born in Paris, his father made the tragic mistake of moving the family back to Krakow in 1936 ("Not the best decision,"[9] he quipped to a reporter eight decades later). When asked to clarify his nationality by TV talk show host Charlie Rose, he responded, "In my soul, I'm French. In my heart, I'm Polish, I think."[10]

He was six years old when the war began. Though his parents were "atheist or agnostic" and his mother only half-Jewish, they were soon herded into the ghetto. After spending his life savings to find a family who would look after his son—and soon farm him out at a profit—Polanski's father surreptitiously snipped a hole in the barbed wire fence the day the ghetto was liquidated and said goodbye.

The boy stayed with a succession of families in the country, adopting the surname Wilk and pretending to be Christian. Soldiers used him for target practice, and he was later injured in an air raid and beaten by a thug, but ultimately, he transcended the brutality and deprivation of his childhood. Although he would be reunited with his father after the liberation, his mother (then pregnant) died in Auschwitz. "Roman is a survivor," his friend Victor Lownes once said. "The real difference between Roman and people like you and me is not that he can survive disasters and you and I can't, but that he somehow expects them."[11]

The future filmmaker stumbled onto his vocation while delivering a comic monologue over a campfire, during a stint in the Boy Scouts. When he was subsequently invited to a radio station to view a children's show, he boldly told producers it stunk because the kids sounded phony; asked to recite something, he performed the monologue and was hired to appear on the program. The woman in charge turned out to run a local theatre group, and the 14-year-old ended up on stage. As a Russian peasant boy captured by the Germans in V. P. Katayev's *The Son of the Regiment*, he had his first real taste of success.

Polanski performed in the theatre for six years but never had any training. He was rejected three times in his bid to enter acting school. He enrolled in Krakow's School of Fine Arts despite its elitist reputation and began to develop a talent for drawing that had surfaced by then. Here he discovered such "unofficial" art movements as cubism and surrealism thanks to teachers who left open books of reproductions lying around. He would later remark, "It's difficult to imagine but it was a shocking and incredible concept to take in: artists could deliberately distort reality for the sake of pleasure."[12] He also began reading the work of writers like Franz Kafka and Samuel Beckett.

Expelled from art school by an eccentric teacher who took an aversion to him, he was so distraught, he contemplated suicide before managing to get a high school diploma. He won a small part in a movie, "an insipid propaganda exercise . . . like all Polish films at the time,"[13] during which he met director Andrzej Wajda, whose planned contribution to the picture was eliminated. Called up for the draft but deciding he'd prefer prison, he was awaiting arrest— while contemplating various means of escaping to the West—when he got a call one night in 1955. Wajda was making his feature film debut, *A Generation* (*Pokolenie*), and had a major role for Polanski.

On the advice of one of the founders of the state-of-the-art National Film School in Łódź, he tried his luck and got in after passing a rigorous 10-day entrance exam. He studied everything there from still photography and art direction to music and literature. Polanski's surreal student short, *Two Men and a Wardrobe* (*Dwaj ludzie z szafa*, 1958), was his first film to be shown publicly and received five international awards, including the Bronze Medal at the Brussels Film Festival, and the Golden Gate Award at the San Francisco International Festival.

"The school was a true haven, a refuge of peace—both politically and culturally . . . everything was geared toward a single goal: the efficient schooling of professional filmmakers." He and his fellow students didn't appreciate it at the time and "never stopped complaining about how much time we were wasting—and those five years did seem like a very long time. But I quickly realized how much I actually owe to the school. There's no doubt it's where I learned my job."[14]

His diploma film, *When Angels Fall* (*Gdy spadaja anioly*), featured a young lady soon to become the first Mrs. Polanski, Basia Kwiatkowska (later Barbara Lass). The marriage was short-lived but his first feature, *Knife in the Water* (*Nóz w wodzie,* 1962), a product of the same period, would become the first Polish movie to win an Oscar nomination for Best Foreign Film. A three-character chamber drama on a sailboat where the sexual tension is never far from the surface, the film also earned a BAFTA Award nomination.

The script was initially rejected until Polanski and cowriter Jerzy Skolimowski "re-wrote a couple of scenes, and gave it a little bit of social background—bullshit, mainly."[15] The picture, which has been compared to Jean-Paul Sartre's *No Exit*, would provide the first example of his fascination with "the behavior of people under stress, when they are no longer in comfortable, everyday situations where they can afford to respect the conventional rules and morals of society."[16]

Polanski and his first wife, Barbara Lass, at a club in Gdansk, Poland. AGENCJA
FORUM/ALAMY STOCK PHOTO

The female lead could not emote, and "the actress who dubbed her part thought the film was a piece of shit,"[17] recalled Polanski. The movie was condemned for showing decadent behavior but quickly won renown for its director. "It appealed to people in the Western world because it is so different from any other Polish film. It came as a surprise,"[18] said Skolimowski, who convinced Polanski to condense the action into one 24-hour period.

The filmmaker rejected the idea of a US remake of *Knife in the Water* with Elizabeth Taylor, Richard Burton, and Warren Beatty as a ludicrous idea, despite the fact nobody would fund the films he wanted to make. Instead, he ended up in London, where he would direct a film about "the disintegration of a girl with mental illness,"[19] titled *Repulsion*. "I knew a girl in Paris a little like this one: extremely timid, shy, blushing, who rarely spoke . . . she wasn't normal sexually, she was so repressed."[20]

Repulsion reverts to the predominant influence of his early short films, when "I saw everything in the mirror of surrealism."[21] He proves the point straight away with his directorial credit bisecting Catherine Deneuve's eyeball, unmistakably suggesting the opening scene of Luis Buñuel and Salvador Dalí's *Un Chien Andalou*.

The film went over budget, as had its predecessor, engendering a reputation that would persist. "I am known as an expensive perfectionist," Polanski admitted. "Truth is, sometimes a certain scene is not quite within your vision correctly yet, but you don't know why, so you must do fifty takes to find out."[22] In the end, he made the film he wanted to make: "If every scene is controlled, every movement planned, every gesture directed, there's nothing but contrivance. I shot *Repulsion* in a way that felt right to me. The film taught me a lesson about just how far one can go with realism."[23] The prospective success of his psychological horror film would ensure financing for *Cul-de-Sac*, after years of rejections.

SETTING THE WHEELS IN MOTION

STARTING FROM SCRATCH

Polanski stood at the edge of a precipice in 1962. His first feature film, *Knife in the Water*, was a flop in its Polish premiere—a snub he was never to forget. His first marriage, "a very traumatic experience"[1] with budding film starlet Basia Kwiatkowska, had fallen apart. Relocating to his native Paris, he saw promise in the ripple effect of the French New Wave, a phenomenon that caused producers to gamble on unknown talents. He began "hustling for film work, learning the hard way how films in the West got made—or rather, how most of them didn't."[2]

A casual invitation to a cocktail party from New Wave producer Pierre Roustang, a gathering where he knew almost no one, proved fortuitous. It was there the earnest and enthusiastic young man met Gérard Brach, a kindred spirit who had just endured a messy divorce himself and was equally broke. The pair became inseparable friends from their first meeting. Brach would provide the solution to Polanski's realization he lacked the discipline: "to sit down every day to write."[3]

A native of Brittany, Brach (1927–2006) contracted tuberculosis when he was 18 and endured five years in a sanatorium as a result. After he recovered, he worked as a runner and production assistant for Roustang; he also played a bit part in in his pal Jean-Luc Godard's *Breathless (À bout de souffle)*. He was unhappily employed as a press officer for 20th Century-Fox when he met Polanski and

Polanski and longtime collaborator Gérard Brach at work on Cul-de-Sac. RUE DES ARCHIVES 3 BIS RUE PELLEPORT PARIS/GRANGER

discovered they shared an absurdist sense of humor and a passion for surrealism.

"I didn't make any money on *Knife in the Water,* and we were living in little hotels and places like that," the director recalled in a *Playboy* interview. "Whenever we got together 100 francs, we were happy as kings." The first item on their agenda was invariably "to run to the cinema to see a movie."[4] Polanski and Brach went to the movies in the Latin Quarter virtually every day, and sometimes twice a day, despite a lack of funds.

Roustang, who had brought Basia to Paris to appear in a picture a few years previously when she and Polanski were first married—and may have harbored a secret passion for her—unwittingly set the wheels in motion for what the director has often called his best film. *If Katelbach Comes . . . (Si Katelbach Arrive . . .),* which would eventually become *Cul-de-Sac,* could not have been further from the producer's mind, however. What Roustang commissioned Polanski to write was the tale of a Polish girl who journeyed to Paris and fell for a Frenchman.

The fledgling filmmaker thought the idea wholly predictable but was in no position to refuse the job. He took a stab at a treatment and showed it to Brach, who was equally unable to muster enthusiasm. They tried knocking it around, but their efforts proved futile, until Roman proposed they put the producer's idea aside and write an original, "whatever we wanted to, just what we would like to see on the screen. Completely disconnected things, just feelings and characters."[5]

The pair made their first sale to Roustang with a segment for the anthology film *The World's Most Beautiful Swindlers (Les Plus Belles Escroqueries du Monde)*, after their dream project failed to promptly find a buyer. Another project for Roustang followed, the unproduced *Chercher la Femme*, along with director Jean Léon's *A Taste for Women* (1964).

Brach once clarified their creative process for an interviewer. "When I work with Polanski, I'm the one who writes it down from our conversations and one tries to render the most faithful way possible what he wants to put in images, and I have to recommence dozens of times. We speak, he goes away and lets me work by myself and when we come together, there are twenty or thirty pages; we discuss, we walk, I take notes, he listens to music or goes away *je ne sais quoi*, and I continue."[6]

His friend and collaborator lacked Polanski's film school education but proved a fast learner. They began the *Katelbach* project with no sense of direction. "We had absolutely nothing, not even a structure for the story," the director recalled. "All we wanted to do was to get on and write something."[7] They jumped from one idea to another, eventually coming up with a concept: A loudmouth gangster named Richard ("Dickie") and his mortally wounded partner in crime, Albert, are on the run from a botched crime. Dickie seeks help from George and Teresa, a middle-aged man and his much younger wife, whom he ends up terrorizing.

Had anyone asked Polanski what the theme of the movie was at this point, he admittedly would have been unable to respond. After all, there was none; they simply wanted to express their state of mind. "Both Gérard and I had recently been let down by women, and the character of Teresa was born out of a slight need for revenge,"[8] the director noted in his autobiography.

Katelbach was essentially a claustrophobic three-character drama, not unlike *Knife in the Water*. Both were psychological thrillers featuring a couple whose world is turned upside down by outsiders, a scenario Polanski would later return to in *Bitter Moon* (1992). Unlike *Knife*, however, where the stranger accompanies the couple to the lake at their invitation, *Cul-de-Sac* concerned an unwelcome visitor who made himself at home in the couple's domicile.

Although Teresa was inspired by Polanski's first wife, she was clearly cut from the same cloth as Krystyna, her predecessor in *Knife*—an attractive young woman who cuckolds her plain-looking husband. George was modeled on producer Roustang, at least physically; Dickie was based on his friend Andrzej Katelbach, who was renting the filmmaker a bedroom in his small house.

"The plot is conventional, the criminals-break-in-and-terrify-occupants formula of 100 thrillers," as author Ivan Butler has stated, "but the plot is the least part of *Cul-de-Sac*, grimmest of comedies, most hilarious of tragedies."[9] Turning away from the French New Wave, which he criticized for its poor technique and amateurish quality, Polanski turned toward Hollywood film noir for inspiration. Chief among the genre titles that have been cited are John Huston's *Key Largo* (1948) and William Wyler's *The Desperate Hours* (1955), both of which starred Humphrey Bogart.

A MEANS TO AN END

Roustang quickly rejected *Katelbach*, wholly dissimilar as it was from the script he commissioned Polanski and Brach to write. "At best, he said it might make a short,"[10] recalled the director, who groused, "I could not find any money for it; nobody would even read our finished script."[11] Alpha Productions, another company in Roustang's Paris office building, eventually came through and bought an 18-month option on the property. Polanski was so desperate he signed away all rights for a $10,000 advance, 20 percent for a scriptwriter's fee, and the remainder for directing, "against 2% net profit, worldwide, that would accrue to me if the film were made."[12]

Dutch producer Paul Kijzer of Cesar Film Productie then expressed interest in *Katelbach*. Not coincidentally Kijzer was coproducing *The World's Most Beautiful Swindlers*, for which Polanski had cowritten (with Brach) and directed the episode *River of Diamonds (La Rivière des Diamants)* with Roustang's Ulysse Productions and other companies. "Kijzer may produce Polanski's next feature film," *Variety* reported in May 1963. "Main attitude of Caesar [sic] Film production is to find stories that can break even on the home market but have an angle for the world market to start with."[13] Nothing materialized, however.

Despite expectations, things didn't change much for Polanski after *Knife in the Water* aroused considerable interest in him at the first-ever New York Film Festival in September 1963. A black-and-white still from the movie even snagged the cover of *Time* magazine, a break from tradition he failed to appreciate. However, the *Katelbach* script, which he had mentioned in interviews with the press, now drew "a lot of predatory interest." A charming but slippery character who called himself Sy Stewart not only requested a free option on the script, he wanted Polanski to sign a contract stating that he'd been handsomely rewarded for his efforts. "The terms of the contract were so unorthodox that his own lawyer outraged him by begging me not to sign it."[14]

Stewart raised some front money but lost it in a London gambling establishment. Polanski was on his guard when Sam Waynberg of Planet Films GmbH telephoned; Stewart had passed along the number. Nonetheless, the Polish-born producer based in Berlin paid

A youthful Roman Polanski visits the New York Film Festival. PHOTOFEST

$2,000 for a three-month option on the script. Early in 1964, Polanski attended Polish Film Week in Munich where he met another Pole, Gene Gutowski, who expressed a desire to work with him. Gutowski didn't have much of a track record but was determined to form an alliance after seeing *Knife in the Water*.

A man who lived nine lives by assuming the identity of a dead man, Eugene Gutowski (1925–2016) was born Witold Bardach in Lwow, Poland (now Lviv, Ukraine). Using the documents of a laborer who died in an accident, he survived the Holocaust by passing himself off as Aryan and stealing radio transmitters for the Polish underground—after losing his entire family in the genocide.

Gutowski worked as a counterintelligence agent chasing war criminals, a sculptor, and a fashion illustrator before becoming a film producer. Living the jet-setting lifestyle of an international playboy—as he saw it—he also served as production supervisor on the 1950s TV anthology series *I Spy* before executive-producing *Station Six-Sahara*.

While in New York, Polanski had told *Variety* of his long-range plans. Reasoning it was easier to build an international reputation in France than in Poland, the filmmaker "plans to remain in France for at least two more features," the trade paper reported, "and once he has gained that international reputation, return to Poland."[15] But Gutowski had other ideas. The producer was convinced Polanski's greatest opportunities lay outside France, sensing "the French, insular and chauvinistic as they were, would never give him the chance to make an important picture."[16]

The London-based producer persuaded Polanski England was "the place for him to be and the key to his future and success." As Gutowski recalled: "I said to him, 'Until you make an English-language picture, you won't be in the league.'"[17] The director, having "spent three or four years with Brach, desperately trying to get something going, without any success,"[18] was game. When he arrived in London for the first time in March 1964, a newspaper columnist reported the 30-year-old director "looks like a college boy—small, slight, neat, with primeval shoulders."[19] According to Gutowski, he couldn't speak a word of English.

Hammer Films, the British production house renowned for such low-budget gothic horror movies as *The Curse of Frankenstein* (1957), passed on *Katelbach*, as did the more esteemed firms on London's Wardour Street. The one company interested in making a film with Polanski was Gutowski's "last resort," The Compton Group, headed by Michael Klinger and Tony Tenser.

The son of a Polish tailor, Michael Klinger (1920–1989) made and tested munitions during World War II; he peddled hot dogs and ice cream in London's Soho and worked as a disc jockey for the BBC before becoming a nightclub proprietor and running a chain of cinemas. He then embarked on his career as a producer. A repair technician for the Royal Air Force (RAF) during the war, Samuel Anthony Tenser (1920–2007), found a foothold in the movie business as a publicist. He devised the UK publicity campaigns for several films starring Brigitte Bardot and was credited with coining the moniker "sex kitten"[20] for her before partnering with Klinger to exhibit and produce movies.

Despite the fancy name and a letterhead to match, their company was being funded primarily by a disreputable little enterprise housed in a basement in Soho—then London's red-light district. The establishment, known as the Compton Cinema Club, offered what were then considered porno films. The owners were looking to buy respectability with their profits. The ambitious duo, who had recently gone to New York "on product prowl,"[21] rejected *Katelbach* as had others but expressed a desire to finance a substantially different endeavor.

The sequence of events leading up to *Repulsion* has taken on a *Rashomon* quality, with many versions of who did what. Tenser told his biographer he invited Polanski and Gutowski in for coffee at the firm's London office, having heard about the filmmaker. "I guessed if they were coming to see me then they had gone to everybody else," recalled Tenser. "But Polanski is a name, he is a director that draws the press."[22] Tenser claimed it was he who suggested Polanski write something more commercial, he and his partner having already decided to expand their slate to more mainstream productions.

Klinger had seen *Knife in the Water* and wanted to work with the director, or so his son recalled. "He was well read and cultured and he loved foreign cinema," said Tony Klinger. "When Polanski approached him at the Cannes Film Festival, with what I think was called *Baby Head*, he wanted to make it straight away. I think the original discussion about it was in Yiddish, as my dad's Polish was limited and Polanski couldn't then speak English at all. My dad's French was very poor so it must have been in Yiddish."

"In the original treatment by Polanski and Gérard Brach, the woman was carrying around the remains of her aborted baby's head and not a rabbit. My father was hard core tough, but even he saw that it had to be changed,"[23] said Klinger. "They changed the baby's head into a dead rabbit."[24]

Klinger saw Polanski as "a great new talent, perhaps even a genius, and the company's ticket to the premier league of international film making and worth a potential loss,"[25] said his son, while his short-sighted colleagues focused on the loss and saw little importance in the gains. "MK was the primary and major shareholder and the boss but had allowed Tenser to be presented as a full partner, but the fact was that MK had the final say. Sometimes this rubbed Tony up the wrong way."[26] His father's business partner excelled at promotion and showmanship, not filmmaking, stressed Klinger *fils*. "Tony was a bombastic, fun guy, very much a showman, not really a businessman or a producer, but great at banging the drum!"[27]

In his memoirs, Polanski remembered "exploratory talks" with Klinger and Tenser, neither of whom would consider his pet project. At their behest, he and Brach quickly wrote a psychological horror film about a sexually repressed manicurist left alone in her apartment, slipping into a lethal paranoiac state. "To hook them, the screenplay had to be unmistakably horrific; they were uninterested in any other kind of film,"[28] stated Polanski. "The script was originally called *Lovely Head*; later it became *Repulsion*."[29]

Gutowski had trouble selling the promising young writer-director of *Knife in the Water* even after it garnered an Oscar nomination for Best Foreign Film, he contended in his memoirs; the producer said he suggested Polanski put *Katelbach* on hold and first make a film that would push the envelope, "stretching the limits of what the censors would allow." By way of example, he took the director to see Ingmar Bergman's *The Silence*, in which the star of the film masturbated herself to an orgasm in one scene, then "a screen first and a big audience puller."[30] To that end, Gutowski asserted, he himself commissioned Polanski and Brach to write *Repulsion* before Compton came aboard.

As Polanski recalled it, Klinger came to Paris to seal the deal *after* Compton's favorable response to the script. Tenser claimed the director brought him a synopsis, "probably about sixteen pages, in French . . . my French isn't very good but I got the bare bones of it—and I thought it sounded very good. So I said yes, if Roman directs it."[31] Gutowski remembered going to Cannes with Polanski and Brach and "all working the beach trying to get the Compton boys . . . to come up with the money,"[32] before coercing a decision. Tony Klinger insisted: "Polanski and Brach, presented by Gutowski to my father at Cannes with a treatment. . . . Any other version is incorrect and self serving."[33]

In any event, the titles and taglines of Compton's productions blatantly characterize the company that would provide the wherewithal for Polanski's first two English-language features—beginning in 1961 with *Naked as Nature Intended* ("Not for adults with high blood pressure or low boiling points!"). They followed up with such fare as *That Kind of Girl* ("Never before has the screen presented this daring subject so boldly!") and *London in the Raw* ("The world's greatest city laid bare!").[34] Klinger and Tenser "were in the porn business basically, well, soft-core porn. That was their business," affirmed first assistant director Roger Simons. "The company that made *Cul-de-Sac* was above a cinema where they'd show porn downstairs. We were upstairs doing the preproduction."[35]

Tony Klinger asserted, "Tenser and some other shareholders really resisted the making of both the [company's] Polanski-directed movies and anything with artistic pretentions. The words used were something like, 'Where's the tits and arse in that?' Put more coherently they wanted Compton to continue making exploitation movies and were determined to force the issue."[36]

Michael Klinger later "claimed to have 'discovered' Roman Polanski and produced his pictures. He did neither," stated Gutowski. "All that he and his partner Tony Tenser provided in the end was the money as distributors and not very much of it, at that."[37] Polanski, Brach, and Gutowski agreed to share the "grotesquely low figure" of $5,000 to make *Repulsion* and a percentage of the net, "but I'd have accepted even less for a chance of directing my first feature film in the West,"[38] said Polanski.

For a project born of expediency and written in 17 days, *Repulsion* was both an artistic and financial success. Though Polanski and Brach would upgrade the script, "throughout the making of it, giving it some psychological background to the main character," the director later acknowledged, "I was never very fond of *Repulsion*, it was something to get going."[39]

Polanski and Gutowski fought the partners throughout production over the budget. "We went over-budget right from the beginning—and behind schedule. It was so tight, it was totally unrealistic. In fact, we went 100% over budget. That means that the film cost, I think, £93,000,"[40] said Polanski.

The director and producer continued jousting with Klinger and Tenser for years to attain a piece of the profits they were due. *Repulsion* was admittedly "a means to an end"[41] for Polanski, but it made him a bankable director. It also introduced the filmmaker to many of the individuals who would help him make *Cul-de-Sac*—most notably cinematographer Gilbert Taylor but also editor Alastair McIntyre, associate producer Robert Sterne, and several others who would join him on Holy Island the following year.

Polanski and continuity girl Dee Vaughan on the set of Repulsion. ROYAL INTERNATIONAL PICTURES/PHOTOFEST

WHEELING AND DEALING

THE DEAL

"You will be gripped by repulsion,"[1] proclaimed the sidewalks of Berlin during the 15th annual Berlin Film Festival (also known as the Berlinale). The slogan proved to be truth in advertising, as Polanski's first English-language feature won the Silver Bear Extraordinary Jury Prize at the event, an award it shared with Agnès Varda's *Le Bonheur*. Associate producer Sam Waynberg talked Michael Klinger into financing the director's next picture on the strength of the award, according to Polanski. But the prestigious prize does not appear to have been the trigger. *Cul-de-Sac* began shooting 11 days before the festival commenced on June 25, 1965.

Germany itself threw some money at the movie several months before the festivities, as *Variety* reported in February. "Three full-length films . . . and eight scripts have just been awarded premiums of $50,000 by the West German Ministry of the Interior here . . . each author was paid $3,750. The eight scripts included . . . *When Katelbach Comes*, Atlas Films, from script by Roman Polanski, Gérard Brach and Detten Schleiermacher."[2] The German newspaper *Die Zeit*, reported the money could only be used for filming. (Schleiermacher was reportedly involved in dubbing the German version of the film, *Wenn Katelbach kommt*, in collaboration with Michel Leiner.)

The wheels were already turning on *Cul-de-Sac* when Polanski attended the Cannes Film Festival to promote *Repulsion* late in May. Judged "too grim to be Britain's official entry,"[3] the film was screened privately in what Tony Klinger called "perhaps unofficial market screenings." *Cul-de-Sac* would be shown similarly the following year. "I also remember MK and Tony Tenser creating the first sales booth in the Carlton Hotel and also being the first to leaflet the festival; in my memory it was done because of those films, which MK believed elevated Compton to a whole new level,"[4] said the presenter's son.

Variety's Cannes correspondent noted on June 2 the "trade screening" of *Repulsion* "was one of the few to attract an SRO turn-out.... More interestingly, however, is the fact that negotiations have started for Polanski's next pic, *Cul-de-sac*."[5] But by then the latter was already in preproduction and plans were being finalized. Though the director maintained Compton was hesitant about making a second film with him, the trade paper had first reported the company would produce *Katelbach* (as it was still being called) on March 31.

Repulsion received a star-studded world premiere in London on June 10, four days before the start of principal photography on *Cul-de-Sac*. Catherine Deneuve, the star of the film, was there along with the likes of Michael Caine, Leslie Caron, and Warren Beatty; Donald Pleasence and Lionel Stander, slated to costar in the new movie, were in attendance as well. So big was *Repulsion*'s promise, the deal for Polanski's next picture was made in anticipation of success the previous one had not yet enjoyed.

"MK financed *Cul-de-Sac* because he thought *Repulsion* was a wonderful film and *Cul-de-Sac* would be even better," contended Tony Klinger. "Along with this [were] the preliminary reactions of MK's overseas distribution outlets, [who] also liked the idea and were keen."[6] Indeed, advance sales in Germany, Japan, and South America enabled Compton to make back its investment before the British release of the film.

"Of course the critical reaction for *Repulsion* being positive reinforced MK's already made decision," said Tony Klinger. "MK was so keen he was prepared to take a financial loss if it was necessary. He

KINEMATOGRAPH WEEKLY: JUNE 17, 1965   115

the Berlin Festival

REPULSiON

has its world premiere

Left to right (top): Yvonne Furneaux and Michael Klinger; Michael Caine and Luciana Palucci; Mr. and Mrs. Lionel Stander. Centre: Edina Ronay; Leslie Caron and Warren Beatty; Ken Harper and J. Lee Thompson. Bottom: Catherine Deneuve, Roman Polanski and Jill St. John; Leslie Elliot (Compton assistant managing director); Henry E. Lester and Miss Anita Hoefer

Despite the "Berlin Festival" headline, photos were actually taken at the London premiere, June 10, 1965. COURTESY OF SCREEN INTERNATIONAL

was a great fan of European cinema and Roman kind of epitomized a British version of that for MK. It's also hard to remember through the cloud of later Roman self-importance and aggrandizement that he and MK really got on famously all through *Repulsion* and that only began to unravel during the production of *Cul-de-Sac*."[7]

Tony Tenser, whose biographer would assert, "*Repulsion*'s reception at Cannes was enough to bring Klinger to the negotiating table,"[8] was against the new project and unwilling to take the risk his partner was inclined to shoulder. It was Tenser who insisted they had to obtain a completion bond through Film Finances Ltd., "which effectively made Cadre Films [Polanski and Gutowski] solely responsible for any cost over-runs,"[9] noted biographer John Hamilton.

THE BUDGET

Cul-de-Sac was budgeted to the tune of £120,000, per Polanski's recollection. According to author Barbara Leaming, the allotted sum was £135,000. Journalist Derek Malcolm put the final cost of the self-proclaimed comedy/thriller at £150,000. "I believe the original budget was set at 120K but then went up to about 135K during the shoot and all together with the later additions it ended up near enough to 150K so the estimates all have truth within them,"[10] clarified Tony Klinger.

"The whole cost was around $300,000 or $400,000, which for this type of film was very little,"[11] Polanski stated. "It was low budget," affirmed Gutowski. "I recall vultures hanging around."[12] *Le Monde* exaggerated the cost of *Cul-de-Sac* as 100 times more than *Repulsion*. The price tag on his second film for Compton was a relatively modest amount of money in any event, but one Polanski was convinced he would never have found in France. "The French are suspicious by nature. They'll risk their cash only on a sure thing, and it was only in England that I was able to find the backing,"[13] he told an interviewer.

The director's fee was a respectable £10,000. As for the crew, "Gil Taylor would've been the highest paid. I suppose it would've been £200 a week then, it might've been £150,"[14] first assistant director Roger Simons recalled of the cinematographer. "I don't know what Voytek would have been paid, but can hazard a guess," said the production designer's second wife, Fionnuala Kenny. "It would have been about $1400 [£500] by my calculation. I know it provided a handsome down payment for his house. He lived on the per diems—they all did in those days."[15]

"It wasn't an expensive film in terms of crew; I think I got £15 a week being the first assistant on *Cul-de-Sac*, which was nothing," said Simons. "It's a black-and-white film in the mid-sixties so you're not talking great money. Michael Klinger didn't spend big money on movies."[16] In lieu of records that no longer exist, Tony Klinger argued salaries were "all normal industry standard at the time."[17]

"The money was good," said sound camera operator Robin O'Donoghue, perhaps the youngest member of the crew. "We were all paid overtime. I was standing in the sea one day, on the causeway, holding the boom microphone. 'Cut! Okay, next shot.' A man comes over to me, he says, 'Sign here.' I said, 'What's that for?' 'Water money. You get £2 for standing in water.' This was in the days of the strong trade unions. I couldn't believe it, I was nineteen years old, I was getting money everywhere. It was all union rates."[18]

Polanski's tendency toward innumerable takes caused no undue amount of angst for the men who financed the picture. "Myself I didn't see it as being a commercial type of film," said Tony Tenser. "We visited the set a few times, just to see how things were going, just to give him encouragement and to be sure all was going well."[19] Michael Klinger complained on more than one occasion about Polanski's excessive number of takes. "We felt, if he goes that way right through the film, he's going to double the budget,"[20] said Tenser.

Film historian John Hamilton recounted one such visit to the location. All was well, with Klinger and Tenser extracting "a promise from Polanski that he would get the film back on track" before they departed, "but as soon as their car disappeared into the distance Polanski continued exactly where he had left off."[21]

Actor William Franklyn, who played Cecil, remembered Polanski's response to budget constrictions in an interview nearly four decades later. "Roman, as soon as he saw money men, an allergy would develop. And the first time they arrived, on the set on Holy Island, he saw them coming down the path and went, 'Bill, Bill, come with me in the car.' He had this Mini Cooper. I said, 'Where are we going?' He said, 'We're going down on the beach to do tide circles.' And I realized, it was something to do with the producers arriving with the briefcases that made him think, 'I'm going to have people telling me I'm behind, the film is taking too long,' whatever it was. And that was his way of getting rid of his angst."[22]

Gerry Arbeid, who served as technical manager for Compton-Tekli, the production company, recalled "screaming rows" that took place between Polanski and Klinger every day during the filming of *Repulsion*. "The sparks flew from both of them, really. On one occasion, Michael came on the set and they were, they were filming and filming, they were into heavy overtime and he went to the camera, he just went and took the film out of the camera and he said, 'That's it, everyone go home.'"[23]

The filmmaker's union with the Compton Group was an uneasy alliance. "They left me alone as far as the artistic side of it goes but I had those guys on my back telling me about the budget," said Polanski. "It was getting on my nerves. I was certainly tense and uptight."[24] The financiers began making inflammatory statements to the press before *Cul-de-Sac* even wrapped production. A *Variety* report on the Berlin Film Festival in July 1965 contained the following tidbit: "Asked what it cost to hire Roman Polanski (director of *Repulsion*), Compton topper Michael Klinger is reported to have answered, '10 years of my life.'"[25]

For his part, Tenser told *Variety*, "Polanski is making another film for us at the moment called *Cul-de-Sac*. I don't know whether he will make a third for us. We hope so, but his budgets keep rising. But we gave Polanski a big break. . . . *Knife in the Water* didn't make any money and people were chary of giving him another chance. We took that risk and it has paid off handsomely."[26]

As Tenser later recalled, "All our problems came over the budget." Using Gutowski as "the go-between" with the director "may have been a source of friction," he acknowledged. "We had no quarrel with Gene of course but he had to stick up for his partner and we simply didn't want to go over budget. Polanski had his own methods of working and we tried to leave him to it. But . . . we had to handle him very carefully."[27]

When Klinger died in 1989, he was quoted on Polanski in the *Guardian*: "Lovely guy. Talented monster. Doesn't understand money. Won't work with him again."

His son, Tony Klinger, elaborated, "Roman was a young man who ruthlessly only saw what he wanted and his own artistic vision. . . . I remember his first phrase in English after he'd been living in England for a month or two getting *Repulsion* ready was at lunch in Isow's Restaurant [in London]: 'The only reason for schedules and budgets is to bullshit financiers.' It was a warning signal."[28]

Observed Robin O'Donoghue: "I think Roman played on his little boy image sometimes. I noticed he spoke perfectly good English but sometimes [said], 'I do not understand.' To get what he wanted, really. I'm sure he did. Certainly on *Repulsion*, he played on his lack of English. . . . He played a bit on, 'I cannot speak English, I don't understand.' Especially to the producers. He would get what he wanted."[29]

THE SCHEDULE

Preproduction on *Cul-de-Sac* took place in May and June 1965 at the offices of Compton-Tekli Film Production Ltd., 60–62 Old Compton Street in London's Soho district. The planning of the film also involved at least two trips to Holy Island to check out accommodations and organize all aspects of working on location. "We certainly did two or three weeks preproduction," remembered Roger Simons. "To create the schedule is the most important element of pre-production. It takes at least a week to break down the script, and sit with Roman and go through all the elements, the props, discuss [things] with the art department."[30]

The film was planned for a seven-week shoot, as indicated on the Movement Order: "Monday, 14th June 1965—Saturday, 31st July 1965. It is intended to work a six-day week, Monday to Saturday."[31] The first members of the company scheduled to arrive on Holy Island early in June were production manager Don Weeks, production designer Voytek, and art director George Lack.

Polanski, producer Gene Gutowski, and actors Donald Pleasence, Alexandra Stewart (the original Teresa), and Lionel Stander were slated for June 7, to begin rehearsals. Cinematographer Gil Taylor was to come the following day, along with electricians, carpenters, prop men, and various others. The remainder of the crew were to arrive at the end of the week, with editor Alastair McIntyre and his assistant coming the following Monday.

Though the director recalled beginning in August, the first day of filming was June 14, as confirmed by the call sheets in Polanski's own files. Scenes 29–42 of the shooting script were slated with rehearsals beginning at eight o'clock. Stander was to explore the grounds of Pleasence's castle abode, trying to determine if anyone was home. "Weather alternatives" were also scheduled as they would be every day of the shoot, with Pleasence and Françoise Dorléac on call from ten o'clock that day. Scenes 59–65 were slated with the couple puttering about the kitchen, and George confronting Teresa about the meager catch from a supposed shrimping expedition—in reality, a romp in the sand with her boyfriend.

Filming would continue for nine weeks instead of the seven initially planned, per the call sheets. As first assistant director, Simons explained, it was his responsibility "to bring the schedule in on time on a daily basis . . . ensure the day's work goes correctly, be the sergeant major working on the set, and to run the shots on a shot by shot basis. It's quite a job, particularly if you're dealing with a man like Polanski."[32] At the end of the ninth week, Compton simply pulled the plug: "Although Klinger made us pack up and leave Holy Island before the film had been completed to my satisfaction, that was basically it,"[33] the filmmaker recalled.

When Polanski went over schedule, "I offered to put my percentage of *Repulsion*'s profits on the line, and even my director's fee,"[34] he said. As a result, his earnings from his first English-language film were tied up for years. By the time *Cul-de-Sac* was completed, his relationship with Compton was irreparably damaged. According to Gutowski, Klinger and Tenser were ready "to close the picture down, and if needed, replace Roman with another director. Eventually a settlement was reached and secretly Klinger assigned [Roman's] and my share in *Repulsion* to Film Finances, the guarantor, to pay for the overages on *Cul-de-Sac*."[35]

The Holy Island comedy of errors became an eerie precursor to Polanski's *Macbeth* (1971), the filming of which the *New York Times* would describe as "a 25-week nightmare of rain, mud, cast injuries and tension." That picture, a first venture into film production for Playboy Enterprises, went nine weeks over schedule and 20 percent over budget. The filmmaker was nearly replaced. "The Playboy people behaved a little bit like a virgin who was very interested in sex but a little bit scared,"[36] Polanski remarked. He could well have made the same comment about Compton, word for word.

Macbeth would not be the last nightmare, of course. The director was "so traumatized" by the making of *Tess* (1979), "I just didn't want to make films anymore."[37] And his follow-up, *Pirates* (1986), was 28 weeks of agony with a multinational crew who couldn't communicate with each other, and a budget that ballooned from $13.5 million to $33.5 million.

CASTING THE NET

The casting process for *Cul-de-Sac* did not nearly go according to plan, though it's difficult to think of a better ensemble than the international quartet chosen for the leads. And although filming conditions were far from ideal, the performances delivered by one young French actress and three of the cinema's best character actors—one apiece from England, Ireland, and the United States—were arguably among the finest of their respective careers.

Polanski knew exactly what he wanted when it came time to cast the film. He and Brach had carefully described the characters in their script. The director also made sketches of the individuals as he envisioned them. "In terms of casting, I believed then—even more than now—that the most important thing was the physique of the actor. They had to be the way I imagined them."[1]

Where Polanski had cast *Repulsion* himself with the aid of a players' directory, this time around he was assigned a casting director, to whom he provided the sketches. Although he almost certainly knew Maude Spector cast *Lawrence of Arabia* for David Lean, he may have been unaware she had assisted on one of his favorite films, Carol Reed's *Odd Man Out*, early in her career.

George was anything but the typical male lead, a middle-aged protagonist who retires to live in a castle with his trophy wife. Per the shooting script, "He is rather a big man of about forty-eight, nearly bald and with spectacles with thin metal frames. He is rather plump, obviously trying to look sporting."[2] Curiously, the director reportedly intended to cast himself in the role as he first conceived it, his lack of resemblance to the character notwithstanding; "presenter" and financier Michael Klinger apparently vetoed the idea of him doing double duty in front of the camera as well as in back of it—a long-held dream that would have to wait for big-scale fulfillment until the next time around.

"I never saw MK give total autonomy on casting to any director, ever," observed Tony Klinger. "He had a great deal of faith in Roman's directing ability but in the end MK had to make distribution sales around the world and some of these took place before delivery of the film, and that relied on having a cast that people wanted along with them being right for the film."[3]

DONALD PLEASENCE

Armed with Polanski's sketches, Spector quickly secured the services of Donald Pleasence. The actor, who was 45 at the time, was then perhaps best known for his performances in the stage and film productions of Harold Pinter's *The Caretaker* and his scene-stealing role in the World War II prisoner-of-war drama *The Great Escape*. Klinger wanted another Donald for the part—Donald Houston, a Welsh actor who played Dr. Watson in *A Study in Terror*, Compton's "Sherlock Holmes meets Jack the Ripper" tale filmed that spring. He acquiesced to Polanski's preference nonetheless.

Armchair Mystery Theatre made the diminutive Pleasence a household name in 1960, thanks to his role as producer, host, and occasional star of the television program. It was Pinter's *The Caretaker*, however, that cemented his reputation that same year. The play brought him widespread acclaim for his portrayal of Mac Davies, a manipulative old derelict when it opened in London; it then crossed the pond to the Lyceum on Broadway, where it garnered him a Tony nomination. Pleasence, who found himself inspired as an actor by birds and animals, "thought of myself as an alley cat"[4] in the title role.

THE TEAM THAT MADE 'TERROR'

Michael Klinger and Tony Tenser who present the film, and stars John Neville and Donald Houston

Donald Houston (right), first casting choice of Cul-de-Sac *"presenters" Michael Klinger (left) and Tony Tenser (second from left).* COURTESY OF SCREEN INTERNATIONAL

Donald Pleasence in The Great Escape. COURTESY OF SAM GILL/ UNITED ARTISTS

Born October 5, 1919, the North Country boy made his stage debut at the age of seven with the Scunthorpe Players in *Passers By*. At 14, he played Caesar in *Caesar and Cleopatra* at Ecclesfield Grammar School. As a "mad cinemagoer" and devotee of US films in his early teens, "James Cagney was quite an influence on me," said Pleasence, who was impressed by the actor's ability to relax. "If I'm able to relax to start with, I can create whatever tension I need for my part. . . . For me, [acting is] a matter of two things—myself in the part and the part in myself."[5]

The scholarship he won to the Royal Academy of Dramatic Art in London was the first step toward the culmination of a childhood dream. But neither the 17-year-old nor his parents could afford the housing, forcing the school dropout to instead take a position as a booking clerk for British Railways. The job was in the family tradition—his grandfather had been a signalman, his father a stationmaster—but he had set his sights on becoming an actor while growing up in his native Worksop, England, a steel town near Nottinghamshire.

Donald and his older sibling Ralph recited poems in local musical festivals in their teens. Even then he was noted for his diction. "I won a great many prizes; my mother still has a drawer full of them,"[6] Pleasence told an interviewer in 1964.

The aspiring actor abandoned the "habit" when he found work as an assistant stage manager for one pound and ten shillings a week, at the Playhouse on Jersey in the Channel Islands. He was 19 when he made his professional debut there in 1939, in an adaptation of Emily Bronte's *Wuthering Heights*, as Hareton Earnshaw, the nephew of the heroine. Two years later, he married a young actress named Miriam Raymond and started a family—with Angela, the first of five daughters—also in 1941. He made his London debut the following year at the Arts Theatre Club in Shakespeare's *Twelfth Night*.

World War II put Pleasence's career on hold. As a pacifist, he initially registered as a conscientious objector but changed his mind when he decided "the idea was absurd"[7] for a fervent anti-Fascist. He enlisted in the Royal Air Force and flew a reported 60 bombing missions before he was shot down over France. He ended up in Stalag Luft I, a German prison camp run by a "psychotic German killer"[8] where he was beaten and tortured but managed to entertain other prisoners of war by appearing in variety shows and plays.

Awaiting demobilization in 1946, he won the role of Mavriky in Alec Guinness' adaptation of *The Brothers Karamazov*, at the Lyric Theatre, Hammersmith, London; director Peter Brook then tapped him to play the bellboy in the Arts Theatre Club production of Jean-Paul Sartre's *Vicious Circle* (better known as *No Exit*). He followed two years at the Birmingham Repertory Company with a stint at the Bristol Old Vic. "These were my real years of training," he recalled. "I had the opportunity to play all sorts of parts, in both classics and modern plays."[9]

Pleasence made his Broadway debut at the end of 1951 in the company of Laurence Olivier and Vivien Leigh, portraying the Major-Domo in Shaw's *Caesar and Cleopatra*, followed by the soothsayer in Shakespeare's *Antony and Cleopatra*. The following year he took a turn as producer at the Edinburgh Festival, starring in his own adaptation of Robert Louis Stevenson's *Ebb Tide*. He returned to Shakespeare during a "disastrous" 1953 season at Stratford-upon-Avon. "I was too old to go there on the middle level, which is what I did. In a big soap factory like that, I found myself feeling inhibited about acting. . . . I felt enveloped, swallowed up, completely blotted out,"[10] he said in retrospect.

He followed his rare failure at Stratford with his 1954 debut in a medium in which he would find great success. Though his part in *The Beachcomber* (as Tromp, an Indian head clerk) was small, Pleasence found his first film experience "very frightening . . . so much to think about all at once . . . and most bewildering of all, the lack of rehearsal."[11] He appeared the same year in the BBC adaptation of George Orwell's *1984*, in the role of Syme, a government worker; he went on to play Parsons, a character based on Syme, in the 1956 film version of the novel.

The actor played one of his favorite roles, the sophisticated Leone Gola, in Pirandello's tragicomic *The Rules of the Game*. Despite a succession of good reviews, he took a four-year hiatus from the stage in the 1950s, for lack of a project that enticed him. Instead, he focused on the television, where he found he could do quality work without patronizing the audience. He was also seen during that period in a film remake of *A Tale of Two Cities* (1958) as the villainous Barsad, "the first of many well-developed characters that later on would become a sort of trademark,"[12] asserted author Christopher Gullo.

Both industry and public perception of the man changed with *The Caretaker,* a success he repeated on film. When it was released in the United States, retitled *The Guest*, Bosley Crowther of the *New York Times* praised "the brilliant bone-deep acting" of Pleasence and costars Alan Bates and Robert Shaw (re-creating their Broadway roles), with the former "almost too realistic."[13] Not that he was at all certain what to make of the piece at first. "I remember asking Harold [Pinter] early on if 'The Caretaker' was supposed to be funny. I thought it was but I wasn't sure. . . . And Harold answered, 'If it's not funny, it's nothing.' It was like being given the first Chekhov play. It was new."[14]

No longer was five-foot-seven-inch actor with the self-described "duck egg blue"[15] eyes seen as an "ordinary bloke." Better and more varied roles began to come his way, notably the part of Flight Lieutenant Colin Blythe ("The Forger"), in the 1963 film *The Great Escape*. When director John Sturges discovered Pleasence had real-life experience as a prisoner of war—the only member of the cast who could make such a claim—he was invited to examine all aspects of the film production. His understated performance (Pleasence's own favorite among his films) enabled him to stand out amid the distinguished ensemble cast and helped make him in great demand among movie producers in the years to come.

Pleasence was much more slight of build than the character Polanski modeled on French producer Pierre Roustang, whom he described as "a rotund balding man with . . . a distinctly parsonical manner."[16] However, he was inspired casting for the part. George was, after all, a timid, cowardly, effeminate man, consistently mocked and henpecked by his second wife, and cuckolded within the first year of their marriage. Robert Morley may have been a closer match physically, but it's difficult to imagine him or anyone else being nearly as effective in the role; perhaps only Alec Guinness could have come close.

"What I felt all along about George, and what I tried to bring out in performance, was that he had a sort of normal normality," Pleasence told author Ivan Butler. "The more ordinary people are, the more extraordinary they can become at any minute—sometimes turning into animals in front of your eyes."[17]

Pleasence's role turned out to be the easiest of the four characters to realize, and apparently the only one cast by Maude Spector. Polanski may well have seen the actor on stage and had a hand in the acquisition, however. "He was playing in the theatre then so it was easy to see him. And I knew we had the husband," the director told documentary filmmaker David Gregory. "The problem was the gangster, this big, exuberant type of fellow it was difficult to come by in England, and Europe I would say. This sort of Wallace Beery type you would frequently see in American movies."[18]

Richard, the antagonist, was sharply drawn in the script: "He is a giant of a man with a round face, unshaven, thick eyebrows with thinning hair cut crew style."[19] As Polanski has acknowledged, the character of the gangster was inspired by Andrzej Katelbach, the friend who had costarred with him in *The Fat and the Lean*, "a huge, sloppy, boisterous bear of a man."[20] Beery, one of the most unlikely stars in Hollywood's golden era, would have been a perfect fit had he been alive and well.

"If ever a U.S. company were to finance the picture, we used to fantasize, we'd hire Rod Steiger or Jackie Gleason," said Polanski. "British actors in that mold were few and far between."[21] Robert Morley again comes to mind as a logical choice, though his frequent portrayals of kings, colonels and other respectable types would likely have worked against him. At least two other suitable actors would certainly have been familiar to Spector but may have been unavailable: Peter Bull, who portrayed Pozzo in the London premiere of *Waiting for Godot* and the Russian ambassador in *Dr. Strangelove*, and Danny Green, who made a career of playing thugs, most memorably a dim-witted ex-boxer in *The Ladykillers*.

LIONEL STANDER

Polanski and his collaborators were "desperately looking" to fill the role when producer Gene Gutowski called one night and told him to tune in *The Eamonn Andrews Show*, British television's equivalent to *The Tonight Show*. "A burly, gravel-voiced American actor named Lionel Stander was holding forth so volubly that no one else could get a word in,"[22] the director recalled. Polanski decided he was perfect for the part and hired him immediately.

Though most familiar today from his stint as Max in the TV series *Hart to Hart*, Stander was one of Hollywood's top character actors in the 1930s, popular for such films as Frank Capra's *Mr. Deeds Goes to Town* and William Wellman's first screen version of *A Star Is Born*. The 57-year-old performer had only recently begun to resuscitate his career after being blacklisted for more than two decades due to alleged Communist activities.

Lionel Stander in A Star Is Born. SELZNICK INTERNATIONAL PICTURES/UNITED ARTISTS

If Lionel Jay Stander wasn't "the first actor to be blacklisted for political reasons,"[23] as he told a journalist, he was certainly among the earliest to have his name besmirched and his livelihood threatened for participation in social and political causes. "I've always been lefter than the Left, and I worked very closely with the Communist Party during the thirties. But I never joined," he stated to another interviewer, recalling "that day in August 1939, when my agent, Abe Lastfogel, came to me and said, 'Harry Cohn got up at a meeting of the [Motion Picture Producers Association] last night and said that your contract was up for renewal but that he didn't want to renew it because you're a red sonofabitch and that any one who hires you will have to pay $1,000 to the [MPPA]. But don't worry, Lionel, it'll blow over.'"[24] The agent was correct, but it took more than two decades.

The son of a certified public accountant, Stander was born January 11, 1908, in the West Bronx, New York City. Following his first job as an office boy at age 14, he tried his hand at all types of employment. He made his unplanned entry into showbiz when he accompanied an actor friend to a rehearsal of *Him* by e. e. cummings at the Provincetown Playhouse in Greenwich Village—ground zero for experimental theatre. An actor was unable to roll dice to the director's satisfaction "and it turned out no one around could shoot craps except me." He also played a policeman and a character called First Fairy "with rouge and a fairy wand"[25] in his 1928 stage debut.

The neophyte scored his first notable success the following year in a Provincetown revival of Eugene O'Neill's one-act sea plays. "In particular the Yank of Lionel J. Stander in the harrowing death scene of *Bound East for Cardiff* is an excellent example of straightforward, simple acting."[26] noted the critic for the *New York Times*.

Stander found himself much in demand as a radio performer in the 1930s, beginning with a stint in the company of acerbic comedian Fred Allen, on whose show he played a variety of ethnic characters for $15 a broadcast. "Fred liked to say that Lionel was always late for the show because he was a radical—that he was working on a printing press in the basement so he couldn't get to the studio on time,"[27] recalled the comic's longtime staff writer, Bob Weiskopf.

Not counting a reported bit part in a silent movie (*Men of Steel* with Milton Sills), the actor entered films in a series of short subjects made at Vitagraph Studios in Brooklyn. He appeared in *In the Dough* with Roscoe "Fatty" Arbuckle and Shemp Howard, *Salt Water Daffy* with Howard and Jack Haley, and *The Old Grey Mayor* with Bob Hope and other shorts, while being heard regularly on radio with Fred Allen as well as Eddie Cantor, Al Jolson, and Fanny Brice.

The actor shot his feature film debut in New York, playing a poet in Ben Hecht and Charles MacArthur's *The Scoundrel* (1935). Stander was then imported to Hollywood by RKO Radio, which began promptly loaning him out to Warner Bros. and other studios; he quickly found himself in demand, so much so he regretted signing a contract. He was especially wary of being exploited, having helped organize the Screen Actors Guild "when it was dangerous to be a Guild member and when we had secret meetings."[28]

Within a few short and busy years, he was seen in such films as *The Milky Way* and *Professor Beware* with Harold Lloyd, *Mr. Deeds Goes to Town* (as a press agent for Gary Cooper), and *A Star Is Born* (again as a press agent). But he had already begun to draw attention for off-screen activities, supporting a myriad of social causes, and his luck soon ran out.

Stander claimed he was "the highest paid character actor under contract to Columbia Pictures"[29] at $3,500 a week when studio chieftain Harry Cohn branded him "a red." The actor stood up at a union meeting and read the criminal records of leaders of the International Alliance of Theatrical Stage Employees (IATSE), at a time when they were "Al Capone's henchmen in charge of making payments to the mob by producers." A mobster working at Columbia as a producer, so he was told, gave the word to Cohn. The result: "a secret blacklist imposed by the MPPA."[30]

The actor was named a member of the Communist Party in 1940 by an alleged former "chief functionary" of the party, who told the grand jury the Communist Party had organized the Hollywood Anti-Nazi League "as a rich source of funds from motion picture players."[31] Stander denied he was ever a member of the party and was publicly cleared of accusations, but by then he was already largely persona non grata in Hollywood.

Stander managed to win the lead role of J. Riley Farnsworth in a CBS radio sitcom titled *The Life of Riley*, not to be confused with the popular show of the same name starring William Bendix. He also returned to Broadway on the other side of the footlights, taking a financial interest in a drama directed by Orson Welles and coproducing *Brooklyn, U.S.A.* by fellow leftist (and future blacklistee) John Bright and Asa Bordages. The same week the play premiered in

December 1941, he opened in the Broadway show *Banjo Eyes* oppo-site Eddie Cantor.

Fritz Lang's *Hangmen Also Die* (1943), scripted largely by Bertolt Brecht, sans credit, provided Stander with one of his few screen roles during that era. He also obtained a small part in *Guadacanal Diary* but elected to enlist in the Army Air Force to combat the paucity of roles available to him.

Hoping to prove Los Angeles could originate worthwhile the-atre, Stander then joined forces with two colleagues and leased El Patio Theatre on Hollywood Boulevard. After opening with a "mod-ernized version" of *Macbeth* early in 1947, however, the actor was reportedly "rather bitter" about L.A. audiences. "He said had he called it *She Dood It in Scotland,* it would have been a smash hit,"[32] noted a journalist.

Moviegoers saw him in the occasional film during this period, notably a remake of *The Milky Way* retitled *The Kid from Brooklyn* with Danny Kaye (on whose radio show he appeared) and a pair of Preston Sturges comedies, *The Sin of Harold Diddlebock* (reissued as *Mad Wednesday*) and *Unfaithfully Yours.* He was also heard as the voice of Buzz Buzzard in Woody Woodpecker cartoons.

Movie work came to a screeching halt in 1951, drying up for more than a decade. Actor Marc Lawrence told the House Un-American Activities Committee (HUAC) Stander was a member of his Holly-wood Communist "cell" and claimed Stander was "the guy who intro-duced me to the party line."[33] Stander filed a $500,000 suit for slander against Lawrence, who fled to Europe to evade the issue. Stander found himself blacklisted anew, however, with the announcement he was being subpoenaed again.

The actor's eventual testimony to HUAC in 1953 is the stuff of legend. "I know of a group of fanatics who are desperately trying to undermine the Constitution of the United States by depriving artists and others of life, liberty, and the pursuit of happiness without due process of law,"[34] Stander charged, turning the tables on the committee. "I attacked them as being part of a conspiracy to impose censorship on American theatre and film, because as soon as you tell people who they can't and won't hire, you also tell them what they can and can't present,"[35] he told interviewers the year before he died.

Stander, who costarred as Ludwell Lowell, the blackmailing agent in Jules Styne's Broadway revival of *Pal Joey*, was appearing in a road show tour of the musical at the time of his HUAC appearance—until columnist Walter Winchell, who provided information on Stander to the FBI, demanded his removal from the show.

The betrayal was typical of the years of rough sledding Stander endured before he found a personal savior of sorts in the person of Tony Richardson. The British stage and film director (best known for the Oscar-winning *Tom Jones*) cast the actor in an extraordinary succession of four projects: three plays and a film.

First, Stander replaced Peter Bull in the New York transfer of John Osborne's *Luther*. He next jumped into the Broadway premiere of Bertolt Brecht's *Arturo Ui*, a burlesque of Hitler's rise to power with Chicago gangsters paralleling the Nazis. Neither the actor nor the play fared well, however, with the *New York Times* critic finding the parallel "clumsy and ponderous."[36] The director then took Stander to London to appear in Brecht's *St. Joan of the Stockyards* as "a big, bad capitalist,"[37] a triumph for both performer and production. Finally, Richardson broke the blacklist by casting the actor in his film *The Loved One*.

The character of Richard is repeatedly described in the script for *Cul-de-Sac* as "the giant," clarifying the casting of Pleasence as George to heighten the contrast between him and Stander. Similarly, the casting of Richard's partner, Albert, was in keeping with the long tradition of physically mismatched movie teams from Laurel and Hardy to Peter Lorre and Sydney Greenstreet. The script made clear the concept in describing Albert: "He is a small puny individual, who could be any age with a moustache. The thick spectacles denote a short sighted man."[38]

JACK MACGOWRAN

Early in 1965 Polanski caught a production of Samuel Beckett's *Waiting for Godot* at the Royal Court Theatre, his first opportunity to take in the London theatre scene. He found himself captivated by "this marvelous scrawny actor"[39] who played Lucky and invited Jack Mac-Gowran to his house. After conversing at length, the director came to the conclusion they simply had to work together; when Polanski began casting *Cul-de-Sac* that spring, "he was the first person that came across my mind."[40]

Jack MacGowran in The Quiet Man. REPUBLIC PICTURES

MacGowran, a veteran of Ireland's Abbey and Gate Theatres, had played small, in conspicuous roles in such films as John Ford's *The Quiet Man* and Tony Richardson's *Tom Jones*. The 46-year-old actor had been offered a part in a picture that would take him back to Ireland for nine weeks and was about to accept when Polanski invited him to a screening of *Repulsion*. "Jack loved blood and gore," recalled his widow, Gloria MacGowran. "He actually had to look away from the film; he was shattered by it. After that, he had to work with Roman. If he could do that, Jack had to—and Roman's eagerness was a factor as well."[41]

John Joseph McGowran (he later changed it to "Mac," only to have his name misspelled for much of his career) was born on the south side of Dublin, October 13, 1918, a few short miles from where Beckett grew up. The gunfire heard in Dublin streets was not the noise of boys playing soldier but the deadly soundtrack of the Anglo-Irish war. He was being wheeled in a pram one day by his mother when a Black and Tans soldier walked up and jokingly pointed a gun in his face—his only brush with the Troubles so vividly depicted in the plays of Sean O'Casey he would one day act on stage.

The son of a traveling salesman, MacGowran spent his early years as a clerk in an insurance company. Seeking every possible diversion outside the office, he performed monologues in Boy Scout variety shows and did mimicry at parties, but amateur athletics took precedence at that time. He made his stage debut at the ripe old age of 22, in the chorus of a trio of Gilbert and Sullivan operettas at the Gaiety Theatre. When an outbreak of influenza played havoc with a production of John Drinkwater's *Lincoln* at the Dublin Gate Theatre, he jumped at the opportunity to play "practically every part except Mrs. Lincoln, very rapidly and very brilliantly—and literally saved our bacon for that,"[42] said director Hilton Edwards.

After playing a leprechaun in the 1946 Christmas pantomime at the storied Abbey Theatre he was determined to get into the company. The Snitch, as he was affectionately dubbed by fellow actors in reference to his nose, was billed under his Irish name by tradition, Séan Mac Shamhráin. He enjoyed a few successes at the Abbey, notably when he directed *In Sand* by the artist Jack B. Yeats and portrayed an Indian peddler in Bryan MacMahon's *The Bugle in the Blood*. Opportunities to excel were few however, and it became obvious by the end of his third year, his future did not lie with the company. Managing director Ernest Blythe, who "disliked my very guts,"[43] was short and to the point when MacGowran went to air his grievances: "Accch, well you see, your nose is too big. And besides, there are not many parts for Indian peddlers."[44]

The actor studied mime with Etienne Decroux during a sojourn in Paris, years before another former pupil, Marcel Marceau, would inspire actors from around the world to make a pilgrimage to Decroux's studio. He made his film debut in Paul Rotha's docudrama *No Resting Place*, as one of the sons in an itinerant family. It was his next film that made the world outside Dublin aware of him, *The Quiet Man* (1952), in which he played Feeney, Victor McLaglen's obnoxious, toadying sidekick. He was brought to director John Ford's attention by Maureen O'Hara's brother, childhood playmate Charles FitzSimons, who helped cast the film.

MacGowran sought additional work in Hollywood after his last scene was shot at Republic Studios, but he was limited in the parts he could play, as far as producers and casting directors were concerned. His small stature brought him almost nothing but offers to play "a little green man,"[45] which he rejected—only to be imported by Disney seven years later to do just that in *Darby O'Gill and the Little People*. Back home in Dublin, he played more important parts on stage, particularly the Dauphin in Shaw's *Saint Joan* opposite Siobhan McKenna.

He moved to London, where he won plaudits for his performances in a pair of Sean O'Casey plays, as The Covey (the personification of young O'Casey himself) in *The Plough and the Stars*, and cowardly Seamus Shields in *The Shadow of a Gunman*. A small part in a radio play by Beckett prompted him to immerse himself in the author's work. "I was struck tremendously by the writing," recalled MacGowran, who'd never heard of him. "It seemed to me to be profound, and yet ironically funny, in a style I'd never come across before."[46]

The role that would alter his luck in London came early in 1958, the part of cranky saloon owner Harry Hope in Eugene O'Neill's *The Iceman Cometh* at the Arts Theatre Club. Kenneth Tynan praised the "weasel brilliance"[47] of his performance and hailed him as one of the best young actors on the London stage. He followed up this triumph by embodying the slavish Clov in the first British English-language production of Beckett's *Endgame* at the Royal Court. Theatregoers walked out in droves on the lengthy, one-act play, once described by its author as "a chess game lost from the start."[48]

The actor made his Broadway debut as the parasitic Joxer Daly in a musical adaptation of O'Casey's *Juno and the Paycock*, a flop that closed after 16 performances. After Peter Hall assured him he had "the perfect qualities for a Shakespearean clown,"[49] MacGowran and Peter O'Toole nearly drank themselves to death at Stratford in 1960, taking refuge in the bottle to combat the despair of what O'Toole characterized as a "deeply depressing season. . . . We had to suffer with that prick for nine months!"[50] MacGowran's attention-getting role as Partridge, the highwayman, opposite Albert Finney in *Tom Jones* easily overshadowed the stage performances that followed.

A one-man Beckett anthology was not the first project that came to mind when he was asked to do something for the Dublin Theatre Festival in 1962, nor was *End of Day* the actor's idea; his wife Gloria was the one who suggested it. "My idea was to change people's ideas about Jack, to show the different facets of things he could do. It was a totally selfish thing on my part," recalled Gloria MacGowran. "But Jack wanted to show the beauty and the humor in Sam; that was his concern."[51] Donald McWhinnie, who had first introduced Mac-Gowran to Beckett at the actor's timid request five years previously, directed the program.

Early in 1964 in Paris, Beckett directed MacGowran in an English-language production of *Endgame* (opposite Patrick Magee as Hamm) that soon transferred to London and came to be regarded as definitive. The avant-garde drama was not universally appreciated; the drama critic of the *Catholic Herald* attacked MacGowran for making himself "a sort of bishop of the Beckett cult"[52] in his scathing review of the play. A "cult" member in the audience left behind a program with a note scribbled in the margin: "Ah, yes, we see it all now. Sam Beckett is God and Jackie MacGowran is his prophet!"[53]

Late that year the author supervised a revival of *Waiting for Godot* at the Royal Court in London, which featured MacGowran as Lucky, the woebegone slave—a role the former amateur athlete compared to "running a four-minute mile twice in an evening."[54] He followed it with Beckett's first play for television, *Eh Joe*, which cast him as a man tormented by his past and was written expressly for him. The actor was ill content with the two dozen films he had appeared in up to that point, including John Ford's *The Rising of the Moon* (as a moonshiner), and Laurence Harvey's *The Ceremony* (a priest) but David Lean's *Doctor Zhivago* (the stationmaster at Yuriatin) was a new low, thanks to the director's lack of regard for actors, in Mac-Gowran's opinion. *Cul-de-Sac* would prove just the opposite.

With the three key male roles cast, Polanski was then faced with a familiar quandary: finding a leading lady. He and Brach had envisioned the role of Teresa as a distinct contrast to George: "She is beautiful, alive with health and vigour. She is about twenty-four years old."[55] She was also American, according to the shooting script. "I remember we saw quite a lot of young actresses, we also saw some models. We had a hard time finding what we wanted,"[56] the director observed.

The film was reportedly written with Polanski's first wife, Basia Kwiatkowska, in mind. The director initially scripted the female lead as "a character who spoke poor English with a foreign accent . . . just like Basia,"[57] asserted Zofia Komeda, wife of the filmmaker's frequent composer and one of his foremost collaborators.

Kwiatkowska, remarried to actor Karlheinz Böhm (*Peeping Tom*), was reportedly forced to turn it down when her husband would not permit her to take the role. "I had only been married to him a few months and he, and I, both knew the dangers. Romek [Roman] would try to get me back,"[58] she recalled. As a result of her rebuff, "a whole layer of the film was lost—all the nostalgia for a country where the character wanted to go but for some reason was unwilling, all the Polish homesickness was lost because Basia wasn't in it,"[59] Komeda told Polanski biographer John Parker.

The filmmaker contemplated using a complete unknown in Charlotte Rampling, who had done uncredited bits in a pair of films directed by Richard Lester, *A Hard Day's Night* with The Beatles and *The Knack . . . and How to Get It*. But she had been signed by John and Roy Boulting, who had put her under contract and starred her in a film awaiting release.

Pleasence, who "had the script for several months" while making *Fantastic Voyage* in Los Angeles, was unprepared for the situation he found on his return to England. "I went back for what was supposed to be two weeks of intense rehearsal, only to find out we didn't have a leading lady," he recalled in an interview. "Polanski tried to get a Czech actress, then he wanted Tuesday Weld and she was unavailable."[60]

Barbara Bouchet, a young starlet born in Nazi-occupied Czechoslovakia, was apparently the Czech actress in question. She had recently signed a contract with Otto Preminger, from whom Polanski attempted to borrow her—as Pleasence reported to *Variety* columnist Army Archerd from location. Bouchet visited London where she tested for Michelangelo Antonioni's *Blow-Up* and possibly *Cul-de-Sac*; Polanski had seemingly encountered her at the recent Cannes Film Festival.

Ultimately, none of the more than 200 actresses and models he tested "had the requisite acting ability," Polanski noted in his memoirs, "though Jacqueline Bisset's outstanding beauty made me think twice."[61] Winifred Jacqueline Fraser Bisset, who had played an unbilled bit in *The Knack* alongside Rampling, had met Polanski when he was filming *Repulsion* in London; she was happy to be cast in a small part, rather than the lead.

Jacqueline Bisset in Cul-de-Sac. CONSTANTIN FILM

"I'll never thank him enough, because it's very dangerous to be faced with an important role when you're inexperienced—if you blow it, it could be the end," she later said. Filming proved educational: "I spent every second of my free time watching, watching, watching. Roman directed and I'd sit nearby learning."[62] Bisset would likely have had issues with the nude scenes Polanski intended, had they been discussed. As she told one interviewer, "I'm one actress who genuinely hates to take her clothes off in films."[63] (Mia Farrow subsequently refused to disrobe for *Rosemary's Baby*, requiring the use of a body double; Tuesday Weld declined to do a nude sleepwalking scene for Polanski's *Macbeth*, which would begin filming without the femme fatale role cast.)

The signing of French-Canadian actress Alexandra Stewart, who had appeared in Preminger's *Exodus* and more recently Arthur Penn's *Mickey One*, brought the search for *Cul-de-Sac*'s leading lady to a halt, at least temporarily. "She seemed to fill the bill, so I started rehearsals with her and the two men, only to find she looked too wholesome and healthy to play the offbeat, slightly kooky role of Teresa,"[64] recalled Polanski.

Stewart, who would ultimately characterize the experience as a "painful disappointment," remembered it differently in her autobiography: "My somewhat crazy, unhinged character in *Cul-de-Sac* seduced me a lot because it was very different from what I had done up until then. Everything was going well, until the day I committed an enormous blunder." The actress ran into Françoise Dorléac in London and "found my *Cul-de-Sac* character looked strangely like Françoise." When she told Polanski of her revelation, she said, he decided she was exactly right. "I was so right that Roman broke my contract to give the role to Françoise Dorléac. My agent was furious. 'Couldn't you keep your big mouth shut?'"[65]

"Alexandra, who realized she wasn't right for the part without being told, was big enough to admit it and spare me what would

Alexandra Stewart, the original female lead in Cul-de-Sac.
PARAMOUNT PICTURES/PHOTOFEST

otherwise have been an awkward situation,"[66] Polanski wrote in his memoirs, in an apparent attempt at diplomacy. But it was hardly a case of being big enough or smart enough to give up the role, said Stewart. "Nonsense . . . I had the stupidity to suggest it to him!"[67]

Actress and director remained on good terms following "the misadventure of *Cul-de-Sac*," observed Stewart, who would later appear in Polanski's *Frantic*. Still, she had to admit, it was a missed opportunity and a stellar one at that. "Roman is an extraordinary director of actors. . . . He would have taught me my profession like no other if I had kept the role of Teresa."[68]

FRANÇOISE DORLÉAC

Whether or not Pleasence was aware of the circumstances behind Stewart's departure is unclear. His recollection of what happened next seems to favor Polanski's version of events. "He called Catherine Deneuve in Paris and she was working on another film but said to look up her sister," remembered Pleasence. "Françoise Dorléac was cast two days before we started shooting."[69] Deneuve has stated she and Dorléac were never rivals for the same role. Her reported response to the casting choice: "What a perfect part for Françoise."[70]

Françoise Dorléac in Where the Spies Are. COURTESY OF SAM
GILL/METRO-GOLDWYN-MAYER STUDIOS

Dorléac was no stranger to Polanski. The filmmaker was socially acquainted with the 23-year-old star of François Truffaut's *The Soft Skin* (*La Peau Douce*) and Philippe de Broca's *That Man From Rio*, courtesy of Deneuve; they had even been photographed dancing together one evening in a Paris nightclub. The sisters had attended the Cannes Film Festival in May where they met up with Polanski, all three unaware the director would soon call on Françoise.

Said Deneuve in retrospect: "I think Roman Polanski is an amazing director. But Françoise did not need my advice for *Cul-de-Sac* ... what I knew is that not only is Polanski a great filmmaker and a true director of actors, [but] he also has a lot of humor. I was sure that humor would unite them and things would work well between Françoise and Roman."[71]

The daughter of actors, Françoise Dorléac was born in Paris March 21, 1942, the second of four girls. She attended convent school and initially desired to become a nun, but the family vocation proved irresistible. Even as a child she earned pocket money by dubbing voices in films, pressed into service by her father, then the dubbing director at Paramount Pictures. (Her mother dubbed Olivia de Havilland and other actresses in French versions of US films beginning with the advent of sound.)

At age nine, Dorléac was cast in a stage production of *The Power and the Glory* with legendary French actor-director Louis Jouvet, but he unfortunately died during rehearsals. She was schooled professionally at Le Conservatoire national supérieur d'art dramatique and modeled for Christian Dior.

The actress was just shy of 18 when she performed the title role in a revival of *Gigi* (1960) at the Théâtre Antoine. Her feature film debut came the year before in *Wolves in the Sheepfold* (*Les loups dans la bergerie*), but it was in Norbert Carbonnaux's forgotten 1962 film *The Dance* (*La Gamberge*), where she first left her mark. Here she found "her first register, the playful fantasy ... alternately frivolous, goofy, carefree, joyful, ultimately young and self-confident . . . seductive and distant,"[72] *Le Monde* observed in a posthumous appreciation.

The actress enjoyed a taste of success in the zany spy spoof, *That Man from Rio* (1964). She didn't have a great deal to do as Jean-Paul Belmondo's archaeologist girlfriend, Agnès, other than play the victim—getting drugged, hypnotized, and kidnapped in the process—but did it all with panache, notably when she danced the samba in one scene. *Le Monde* felt she rediscovered "a little of the art of a Katharine Hepburn at the height of American comedy. Flirtatious, worldly, unbearable and irresistible."[73]

Though she esteemed Hepburn and Kay Kendall, her ambition was "to be like the one and only Garbo,"[74] stated Dorléac. "Being both very sophisticated and very good at comedy, she admired the stars who can play on several registers and she could not find among French actresses a real model," said Deneuve. "She always tried to excel, to achieve things beyond her means."[75]

Her favorite motto: "Be realistic. Ask the impossible."[76] Indeed, she seemed to hold herself to a high standard. "It's very hard to remain a woman," she asserted. "I hate what they call 'nice, charming.' I want to be fantastic! A girl must have mystery."[77]

She appeared in three additional films the same year as her breakthrough in *That Man from Rio*, including a bit in Roger Vadim's adaptation of *La Ronde*, and Edouard Molinaro's *The Gentle Art of Seduction* (*La chasse à l'homme*) with Belmondo and Deneuve. Most memorably, Dorléac was seen in *The Soft Skin*, which Deneuve has called "The film most faithful to what Françoise was."[78] Dorléac, who played a flight attendant openly having an affair with a married man, wasn't too fond of the character at first but felt "Nicole ended up resembling me. François [Truffaut] made her talk like me, tell stories that happened to me, with slight changes. This explains why today I'm not so sure about not liking her anymore."[79]

Though there was never a professional rivalry between Françoise and Catherine "because we were too different,"[80] they unwittingly found themselves in competition with each other when *The Soft Skin* and *The Umbrellas of Cherbourg* were both shown at the Cannes Film Festival in 1964. The latter won the Palme d'Or and launched Catherine to stardom—a triumph tarnished by Françoise's disappointment when the Truffaut film was panned, though it later garnered accolades.

To exacerbate the situation, *Umbrellas* led to numerous offers for Catherine, who "did not want to do cinema at all," while Françoise found her career at a standstill: "And to me, who wanted to make it, who was craving to make it, nobody offered anything."[81]

On Deneuve's recommendation, Polanski signed Dorléac to play a part in *Cul-de-Sac* as promiscuous as her sister's character in *Repulsion* had been repressed. "Although I hadn't wanted a French girl to play Teresa, the script could easily be adapted," he recalled. "I hired her without a test, and we were ready to roll."[82]

With filming slated to begin almost immediately and everything arranged, there was no time for revisions; Polanski would simply adapt on the fly as the shooting schedule demanded, improvising as he went.

Deneuve had rewarded the filmmaker with a stunning performance in *Repulsion*, a feat he no doubt hoped Dorléac could duplicate. Polanski's choice had made all the difference the last time around, though Michael Klinger considered Deneuve an unnecessary splurge. The director was less than enamored of Klinger's first pick for the part in *Repulsion*, Francesca Annis, though years later he would cast her as Lady Macbeth. "This was before she had her nose job," asserted Tony Klinger, "and Roman, in a stage theatrical whisper turned to MK and said, 'Why did you bring me Pinocchio?' He could be very cruel, but she heard him and was with the plastic surgeons pretty soon after that."[83]

THE SUPPORTING CAST

To play the small part of Teresa's lover, Christopher, Polanski chose a young man he first met when Iain Quarrier crashed a party he threw, arriving with a girl on each arm. The uninvited guest was "very much at the center of the London scene, and I profited a lot from his social know-how—his almost uncanny knowledge of who, where and what was 'in' at any given moment."[84]

As Gutowski recalled, "He was a layabout, a social friend of Roman's from swinging London. A very handsome guy. Neurotic. And I rather liked him."[85] Quarrier, who wanted to be an actor, was delighted when Polanski selected him for the part. The requirements were few; he had only to "look British" and teach himself to walk on his hands. Indelibly associated with the London of the Swinging Sixties, Iain Quarrier (1941–2016) was actually a native of Montreal, Quebec. He made his inauspicious debut in the small indie movie *The Fledglings* (1964).

The cast of Cul-de-Sac, *as seen in a promotional booklet.* COMPTON FILMS

Maude Spector, who reportedly first suggested Sean Connery for the role of James Bond, earned her paycheck helping the director to flesh out the supporting cast with a bevy of experienced character actors he judged "excellent." Renée Houston, who played a beauty parlor client (whose finger is accidentally sliced) in *Repulsion*, was selected as Christopher's mother. Nearing the half-century mark in her career, she had enjoyed an extensive run in variety and revue before making her way into film and television.

Befitting the senior member of the cast, Houston (1902–1980) made her stage debut as a schoolgirl in 1916 before most of her fellow cast members were even born. The daughter of variety artists, Caterina Rita Murphy Gribbin was born in Johnstone, Renfrewshire, Scotland. She enjoyed a career in the music hall with her sister Billie in the 1920s and '30s, appearing as The Houston Sisters (using their mother's maiden name) at variety theatres throughout Britain. Queen Mary once reportedly removed her gloves to shake hands with Renée and Billie after a Royal Variety performance. The sisters performed in pantomimes together and made their film debut in a 1926 short with a musical score; they also appeared in the silent *Blighty* and *Happy Days Revue* (as a sister act). Houston made her musical comedy debut in *Love Laughs—!* at the London Hippodrome and won acclaim for her performance in the revue *Sauce Tartare*. Prior to *Cul-de-Sac*, her films included *The Belles of St. Trinian's*, *The Horse's Mouth*, *Carry on Cabby*, and *Secrets of a Windmill Girl* (for Michael Klinger and Tony Tenser).

Geoffrey Sumner, chosen to play opposite her as Christopher's father, had logged more than three decades on stage and film. A native of Ilfracombe, Devon, Geoffrey Sumner (1908–1989) made his stage debut in 1931. He appeared regularly in London's West End throughout the decade. During World War II he gained renown for his comedic impressions for British Pathé of radio broadcaster William Joyce alias Lord Haw Haw, infamous broadcaster of Nazi propaganda—a role Polanski was most likely unaware of but would no doubt have approved.

Fox Movietone News employed Sumner as a legit newsreel commentator. His films included *Old Mother Riley in Society*, Anthony Asquith's *While the Sun Shines*, a screwball comedy about a radio detective called *Helter Skelter*, and *The Flying Eye*; he also wrote and produced documentaries. On television he was seen as Major Upshot-Bagley in the sitcom *The Army Game*, a caricature he repeated in the spin-off *I Only Arsked!*

Marie Kean was cast as George's aptly named friend, Marion Fairweather. A veteran Dublin stage actress, she had worked alongside Jack MacGowran at the Abbey Theatre and occasionally ventured into films. A one-time student of the Gaiety Theatre School, Marie Kean (1918–1993) was recruited for the Abbey in 1948. Billed under her Irish name Máire Ní Chatháin, she appeared in the first production of *All Souls' Night*, an experimental staging of Garcia Lorca's *The House of Bernarda Alba*, and such plays in Gaelic as *Tristan agus Isialt*. Beginning in the mid-1950s, the Rush, County Dublin, native was heard in the long-running radio soap opera, *The Kennedys at Castleross*. In 1963 she was seen as Winnie in the Irish premiere of Samuel Beckett's *Happy Days*.

Robert Dorning, who was slated to play Kean's husband, Philip Fairweather, had performed variously as a musician, a dancer, and an actor in musical comedies as well as crime dramas. The son of a coalmine worker, Robert Dorning (1913–1989) was a man of myriad talents born in St. Helens, Lancashire, England. He studied ballet and joined an amateur operatic society before becoming a prolific British character actor. After serving in the RAF during World War II, he appeared in *The Red Shoes* and other movies. He became more visible on television, especially in series like *Hancock's Half Hour*, *Bootsie and Snudge*, *Pardon the Expression*, and *Q6*.

William Franklyn, cast as the couple's friend, Cecil, was younger and less experienced but had nonetheless essayed a wide variety of roles on stage, film, and TV. Born into a family of actors, William Leo Franklyn (1925–2006) was the son of a celebrated farceur. After making his debut as a teenager in *My Sister Eileen* at the Savoy Theatre in his native London, he served as a paratrooper during World War II. One-time straight man to legendary British comedian Tommy Trinder, Franklyn made his film debut in the Ealing melodrama *The Secret People* (1951), following it with such movies as *Above Us the Waves*, *Quartermass II*, and *Pit of Darkness*, in which he starred. He made a bigger impact on television, notably as British agent Peter Dallas in the 1960s series *Top Secret*, fighting crime in Buenos Aires; he also appeared in such programs as *Scarlet Pimpernel* and the BBC's satirical *That Was the Week That Was*.

Jacqueline Bisset (1944–) was called on to play the small role of Cecil's girlfriend Jacqueline, the Weybridge, Surrey, British native's first speaking role. The character's name may have been a coincidence; she didn't quite match the part as described in the script, "a young girl who is rather a beatnik."[86] Trevor Delaney, who began his short-lived career as a dancer, was cast as the Fairweathers' mischievous son Horace in his apparent film debut. Casting director Maude Spector also placed him in *The Spy with a Cold Nose* (1966) and *Casino Royale* the following year.

Save one exception, none of the principal actors in *Cul-de-Sac* had ever worked together before—Pleasence and MacGowran had filmed *Manuela* in Spain a decade previously—nor would they in the future. That the stars would never associate professionally again was doubtlessly a source of mutual satisfaction, given that they were barely on speaking terms by the time the film wrapped.

Polanski would have less aggravation casting his next picture, *Dance of the Vampires*. He wrote one of the starring roles for himself, a bumbling assistant to a vampire hunter, and though he eschewed screen credit he took his turn in the spotlight with comic perfection. For his leading lady, however, he ended up not with his actress friend Jill St. John as planned, but the protégé of producer Martin Ransohoff—a neophyte being touted as a sex symbol and groomed as "the successor to Marilyn Monroe," despite her contention she was "the most unsexy thing that ever was."[87] The director's first meeting with Sharon Tate was "a case of instant hate," as far as she was concerned. Small wonder, after an hour of unkind remarks about how unsuited she was for the part. "That's the craziest nut I ever met," she told Ransohoff after their dinner meeting. "I will never work with him!"[88]

St. John was suspicious of Ransohoff from the beginning. "I think he's phony," the future James Bond girl told the director. "I don't trust him."[89] Nonetheless, after a second dinner with Tate at the behest of the producer—who had tried to force the actress on director Sam Peckinpah for the role of Steve McQueen's girlfriend in *The Cincinnati Kid*, before firing Peckinpah off the film—Polanski invited Tate to his apartment. He lit some candles and then left her alone. "A short while later he came storming into the room like a madman and he was wearing a Frankenstein mask," recalled the actress. "I let out a blood-curdling scream, and while I was still crying from the scare, he was calling Ransohoff to tell him that the part in the film was mine."[90]

RECRUITING THE CREW

Voytek was an award-winning designer of stage sets, costumes, and masks when he signed on as *Cul-de-Sac*'s production designer. Polanski no doubt felt a kinship with his fellow Pole, a former prisoner of war who was decorated for his part in the Warsaw Uprising during World War II. Known professionally by his nickname, Wojciech Roman Pawel Jerzy Szendzikowski (1925–2014) had never worked on a film when he interviewed for the job in a London hotel.

"The interview was conducted in three languages, English, Polish and French. Voytek spoke all three with ease," recalled his second wife, Fionnuala Kenny. "It was not the usual interview. The producers asked some questions while Polanski, according to Voytek, looked bored and restive. Suddenly, he fired a question at Voytek, in Polish: 'What have you got in your pocket?'"

"Anyone who had ever been in combat or in a camp valued the knife more than any other possession," said Kenny. "Voytek always carried a knife—an Opinel, the French folding knife with a collar. For everyday use, Voytek carried one with a six-inch blade; he kept it as sharp as a lance. He reached into his back pocket and pulled out his knife and put it on the table in front of Polanski. Without a word, Polanski opened his knife and set it, blade open on the table. The way that Polanski positioned the knife let Voytek understand that they were to play a game in which you hit the blade of your knife with the side of your hand, send it spinning, then catch it by the hasp [clasp] before it hits the ground."

Production designer Voytek. COURTESY OF
FIONNUALA KENNY

"Voytek felt two conflicting thoughts—Polanski was notoriously competitive and usually won. But Voytek had excellent reflexes. If he beat Polanski, would he lose the job? Polanski counted down and both knives went spinning in the air. Voytek caught his a split second before Polanski did. Polanski looked at Voytek and said, in Polish, 'You've got the job'—then went back to looking bored while the others asked the usual questions."[1]

The designer was an aficionado of Polish cinema who had much admired *Knife in the Water*. Clearly, he and Polanski were destined to work with each other. "There was definitely a meeting of minds," said Voytek's son, Joe Roman. "From what I understand the main link between Polanski and Voytek was surviving Warsaw, the Uprising and Voytek's part in fighting in the resistance and being awarded the military cross. I think for the rest of his life he enjoyed a unique sense of humor fueled by the absurdities of class, politics, and the lessons he learned witnessing the horrors of war; I guess they both did."[2]

Forced to attend an agricultural school, Voytek secretly studied architecture at his native Warsaw's "underground university"[3] during the German occupation and its attack on Polish culture. He was wounded during the Warsaw Uprising and held captive as a prisoner of war in Germany; after the war he relocated to London, where he attended the Old Vic School of Design. Voytek (as George Devine of the Royal Court Theatre dubbed him) designed sets and costumes for Nottingham Playhouse, Royal Shakespeare Company, Birmingham Rep, and many other theatre companies, his work "often a victory against seemingly insurmountable odds of space or budget."[4]

Voytek may have been introduced to Polanski by Donald Pleasence; the two had become and remained close friends after working on *Armchair Mystery Theatre* for ABC Television. A more intriguing connection is suggested by Polanski's and Voytek's shared affinity for the Theatre of the Absurd—Voytek designed productions of Beckett's *Waiting for Godot* and Eugene Ionesco's *The Bald Soprano* at Nottingham Playhouse and directed *Godot* for London's ABC TV in 1965. Clearly, he was a kindred spirit shaped by the same Eastern European influences as both Polanski and Ionesco.

The designer was not only a newcomer to film. Unlike virtually every other member of the *Cul-de-Sac* crew, he also had no prior experience with the director. Though Polanski would later refer to *Repulsion* as a "work of prostitution,"[5] the picture had given him the chance to collaborate with most of the people who would later help him capture a more personal vision on film. As frustrating as it may have been to put a passion project like *Cul-de-Sac* on hold while he made a work for hire, Polanski benefited immeasurably from the result. *Repulsion* not only afforded him his first opportunity to make a film outside Poland but also enabled him to become far more proficient in English while he was at it.

GIL TAYLOR, CINEMATOGRAPHER

Michael Klinger and Tony Tenser may have been a last-ditch option to finance his first English-language film, but the man behind the camera was Polanski's initial choice, an artist of the first rank. "As I saw it, the only person who could do justice to our black-and-white picture was Gil Taylor, whose photography on *Dr. Strangelove* had deeply impressed me,"[6] the director stated. The esteemed cinematographer, who began working in films at the tail end of the silent era, was much sought after because of his eye-popping work on Stanley Kubrick's Cold War satire as well as Richard Lester's freewheeling *A Hard Day's Night.*

Though Klinger had fought Polanski constantly about expenses on *Repulsion* far exceeding the sexploitation movies he was accustomed to making and objected on the grounds that Taylor was "one

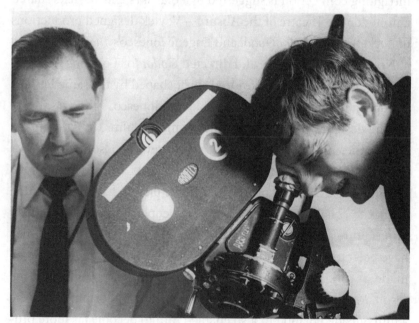

Cameraman Gilbert Taylor and Roman Polanski on the set of Repulsion.
COLUMBIA PICTURES/PHOTOFEST

of the most expensive cameramen in the business," the filmmaker dug in his heels and got what he wanted.

Gilbert Taylor (1914–2013) had to invent on the fly for *A Hard Day's Night*, making it up as he went along, improvising without a proper script as he chased after the Fab Four with zoom lenses on hand-held Arriflexes while dodging crowds of screaming Beatlemaniacs. But for Taylor, who joined the RAF volunteer reserve and flew in Lancaster bombers to photograph the targets of night raids on Germany at the behest of Winston Churchill, the low-budget documentary-style shoot with the lads from Liverpool was a cakewalk by comparison.

Flying behind enemy lines to film for the prime minister and covering the liberation of the concentration camps "certainly made me tougher."[7] But then the movie industry was a tough one, as Taylor well knew. He was displeased with Kubrick for battering him with technical questions on *Dr. Strangelove*, and while his wife Dee Vaughan, the continuity girl on the film, later claimed, "Gil and Kubrick got on terribly well together and had a great relationship,"[8] cinematographer Oswald Morris (*Lolita*) recalled his colleague developed a hatred of the director during the filming. "I sometimes felt as if his hand was on the brush and I was the paint coming off it!"[9] said Taylor, though he acknowledged, "Lighting that set was sheer magic. I don't quite know how I got away with it all."[10]

The son of a builder, the Hertfordshire, British native studied to be an architect. He started operating his uncle's newsreel camera when he was 10, however, and seemed to know instinctively that was his future. "By the time I became a camera assistant, when I was fifteen, I already knew a great deal about the business,"[11] he said. He began his career as an assistant at Gainsborough Studios in 1929, hand cranking a wooden camera on the last two silent films made there; he was a clapper boy on Alfred Hitchcock's *Number Seventeen* (1932). Taylor served as an assistant on Lupino Lane's *Me and My Girl* and other films before becoming director of photography on *The Guinea Pig* and *Seven Days to Noon* for John and Roy Boulting and *The Yellow Balloon* and *Ice Cold in Alex* for J. Lee Thompson.

Taylor thought *Knife in the Water* looked "absolutely dreadful"[12] and debated lighting and lenses with Polanski when they filmed *Repulsion*. Despite his offbeat methods of using reflective light and dismissing light meters, however, Polanski felt Taylor "possessed such an unerring eye that his exposures were invariably perfect." He also proved to be the perfect accomplice in channeling Alfred Hitchcock, intentionally or not.

He hesitated when Polanski again requested him for *Cul-de-Sac* because "I wasn't sure about what Roman was doing,"[13] but ultimately chose it over a 16-week assignment on the James Bond movie *Thunderball*. Taylor later named the two Polanski films (both of which garnered him BAFTA nominations) along with *Dr. Strangelove* his favorites of all the pictures he photographed and told an interviewer he loved working with the director. "Polanski wears you down and brings you to tears, and in the end you do it his way,"[14] he observed in a documentary. Nonetheless, their relationship endured some rough sledding. "I must say *Repulsion* was the most fantastic experience I've had with a cameraman," Polanski said of his first collaboration with Taylor, "and then I took him for *Cul-de-Sac*. . . . Gilbert was a little bit less able on location; also, he had some personal problems of a sentimental nature and he wasn't in the best shape."[15]

"He was a lovely man, a great black-and-white director of photography," recalled *Cul-de-Sac* sound camera operator Robin O'Donoghue. "In those days they had big arc lamps; they used big weights to put on the legs of the arc lamps to stop them falling over. And one of the electricians dropped something on Gil Taylor's foot, so he was limping the whole location."[16]

ALASTAIR MCINTYRE, EDITOR

Beginning his film career as an assistant editor circa 1952, Alastair McIntyre (1927–1986) worked for a decade on nearly two dozen films as a sound editor (*All at Sea, Make Mine Mink*) or dubbing editor (*Room at the Top*, Bryan Forbes' *Whistle Down the Wind* and *The Quare Fellow*). McIntyre, who was then promoted to editor, became another vital member of the *Repulsion* team. Though he earned his first credit in that capacity on *Station Six-Sahara*, which Gene Gutowski executive produced, he was more likely brought on board by Michael Klinger, with whom he worked on two 1964 releases; in any event, McIntyre did his job so well on Polanski's first British film he went on to edit not only *Cul-de-Sac* and *Dance of the Vampires* but three additional pictures for the filmmaker, not counting one Polanski wrote but did not direct (*A Day at the Beach*).

KRZYSZTOF KOMEDA, MUSIC

Perhaps the man behind the scenes of *Cul-de-Sac* with whom Polanski had the closest working relationship was Krzysztof Komeda. There's something poetic about a musically inclined young man who chooses to study medicine and pursues laryngology, devoted to the human organ that produces sound. Because a respectable physician could not play "the decadent music of the West,"[17] Krzysztof Trzcinski (1931–1969) chose the pseudonym Komeda as a guise while pursuing his passion—a passion that first became apparent at seven when he began to play piano in his native Poznan, Poland.

Witold Kujawski, a schoolmate, was already a bass player of some renown when he hipped Komeda to the underground jazz scene in Krakow early in the 1950s. Banned and even persecuted at times, the music could only be played at private homes and parties. Komeda and Kujawski played side by side in Melomani, the first postwar

Writer Marek Hłasko and composer Krzysztof Komeda, right.
BY MAREK NIZICH-NIZIŃSKI—WIADOMOŚCI NR 26/1971/WIKIMEDIA
COMMONS

Polish jazz band; Krzysztof also performed with a Dixieland group, but his growing fascination with modern jazz soon manifested itself in the Komeda Sextet, a band whose music has been compared to the then-popular American group, The Modern Jazz Quartet.

The one-time doctor, who became Poland's top jazz pianist and composer, worked on several of Polanski's short films, including *Two Men and a Wardrobe, When Angels Fall, The Fat and the Lean,* and *Mammals.* The composer also scored Janusz Morgenstern's *Goodbye, I'll See You Tomorrow* and Andrzej Wajda's *Innocent Sorcerers* (both of which featured he and Polanski in the cast).

Though Komeda was "almost standoffish at first, as cool as his music," said Polanski, as they got better acquainted, "I realized that his reserve was a symptom of profound shyness, a veneer that masked the gentleness and high intelligence of the man beneath."[18]

The director wanted Komeda to score *Repulsion* following their collaboration on *Knife in the Water,* "but the British craft unions refused to allow it," said the composer's wife, Zophia Komeda. "But now, after the good reviews for *Repulsion*, his position was strengthened and he could argue with them. He wanted Krzys to write the music for *Cul-de-Sac*, but even then he had to make a formal request, with written reasons several pages long, stating why he wanted to employ a Pole and not an English composer. This time they agreed, but he did not like the British unions very much afterwards."[19]

Hiring Komeda was anything but simple, concurred Gutowski, who recalled that "we worked very hard to persuade the unions in England to allow him to come . . . we had to prove to the unions and to the state department and foreign office that we must have him." It would be easier on *Dance of the Vampires* having previously employed him, said the producer, "but we had to repeat the same process of applications."[20]

For both director and composer, the chemistry between them was sublime. As Polanski told an interviewer, "I would say that when I work with Komeda . . . I exert less influence on other people I work with since he understands perfectly what I want and we communicate very well. I just tell him roughly what kind of music I want for the film, that's all."[21] The composer's biographer, Marek Hendrykowski, observed, "The Komeda-Polanski friendship and creative relationship was unique. They trusted each other in their work and in life."[22]

ASSORTED CREW

Samuel Waynberg (1925–2011), who got his start as co-executive producer of the 1958 German war documentary *He Walked by My Side* (*Er ging an meiner Seite*), served as associate producer on *Repulsion* and Klinger and Tenser's *A Study in Terror* before acting as executive producer on *Cul-de-Sac*. The Polish-born concentration camp survivor also would end up serving as a congenial mediator between Klinger and Polanski.

Bob Sterne, who served as production manager on such films as Kubrick's *Lolita* before acting as associate producer on *Repulsion*, functioned as production supervisor on *Cul-de-Sac*. He was brought to the table as well by Klinger, for whom he had worked on at least four previous films; he was nonetheless "forever torn between his loyalty to Compton and his fast-growing enthusiasm for my way of doing things,"[23] observed Polanski. Production controller Terry Glinwood was similarly involved in four Klinger/Tenser projects prior to the two Polanski films.

Ted Sturgis, whose career stretched back nearly as far as Gil Taylor's, was first assistant director on *Lawrence of Arabia* before serving in the same capacity on *Repulsion* and *Cul-de-Sac*; when he developed a hernia three weeks into production on the latter, he was replaced by his protégé, Roger Simons, as first assistant. "I took over temporarily, and they were going to bring up another first assistant from London. And Roman just said no, I think because he felt he could control what was going on. I was only twenty-two,"[24] recalled Simons, who would work on Polanski's *Macbeth* in the same capacity.

Twickenham Film Studios, which would be used for postproduction, provided Polanski with the sound team for *Cul-de-Sac*, as they had on *Repulsion*. "Roman came to the studio, and effectively he was given a sound crew by the studio,"[25] said Robin O'Donoghue, who served as sound camera operator on both films.

Sound supervisor Stephen Dalby, with whom Polanski had clashed on *Repulsion*, did not reprise his role on *Cul-de-Sac* despite receiving credit on the film. Dalby "wasn't accustomed to my meticulous ways," said the director. "He failed to see why the process [sound mixing] couldn't be rushed, as it was with the average B feature."[26] In a career that lasted more than four decades, "Steve felt he [Polanski] was the only director where the work ended with a poor relationship,"[27] said his colleague, Peter Musgrave.

Recalled O'Donoghue: "Stephen was old school. 'You do it the way I do it.' Roman would have to do what Steve said. There was a young mixer who was Stephen's assistant, Gerry Humphries, who was the same age as Roman. On *Cul-de-Sac*, Roman said, 'I want Gerry to be the mixer in the theatre.' There was a huge kerfuffle about this at Twickenham. At the same time we had Dick Lester, who was also in his early thirties, asking for Gerry to mix the Beatles films. Gerry became Roman's [dubbing] mixer, and Stephen moved to the side as head of sound."[28]

O'Donoghue also remembered the sound mixer on location, George Stephenson, as "a very nice man. He was quite an elderly man but Roman loved him because he cared, he wasn't jaded by having done sound for so many years. He was enthused by Roman's enthusiasm, to get proper production sound."[29]

Script supervisor Diane "Dee" Vaughan, prop man Alf Pegley, and still photographer Laurie Turner all worked on Polanski's first English-language film before signing on for his second. All had worked on at least one picture bearing Klinger's fingerprints—as had hair stylist Joyce James and casting director Maude Spector, who would later rejoin Polanski for *Pirates*. Wardrobe mistress Bridget Sellers was another *Dr. Strangelove* alumni, as was Vaughan.

Camera operator Geoffrey Seaholme had three decades of experience in the industry, including a stint at Ealing Studios, where he worked on such classics as *Kind Hearts and Coronets*. After a falling-out with Taylor on *Cul-de-Sac*, Seaholme was replaced with Roy Ford, who had served as Taylor's focus puller on *A Hard Day's Night*. "Geoff was one of Britain's finest camera operators. And it was accepted if you placed Geoff on a picture, he does have a great liking for a glass of alcohol. . . . He always got the shot but he did like to drink," recalled Roger Simons. "There was a confrontation in the hotel in the evening. Gil came on the next day and said I had to get rid of Geoff; it was pretty early in the film. I believe the reason Geoff got fired was because he either made a comment about Gil's [future] wife or there was a question mark about his volume of drinking. I can't be sure of which one it was . . . but he was drunk all the time, that was the main problem."[30]

Cul-de-Sac art director George Lack began his film career in the postwar era as a draughtsman about the same time Voytek ventured into theatre, reportedly working (uncredited) on *The L-Shaped Room* and *The Servant*, and functioning as assistant art director on *A Hard Day's Night*. Les Bowie had done special effects for more than two dozen horror, fantasy, and science fiction movies, including *Fahrenheit 451*.

One individual who got along well with the crew was "a thin, gangling young man" fresh from Oxford named Hercules Bellville whom Polanski met just as production was about to begin on *Repulsion*. Impressed with his "obvious enthusiasm—and his unlikely-sounding name"[31] despite his lack of a union card, the director hired "Herky" on the spot as a runner, a function he also performed on *Cul-de-Sac*; it was only the beginning of a long working relationship with the filmmaker.

To create the poster art as well as the playful opening credits for *Cul-de-Sac*, the director chose a Polish artist whose absurdist bent matched his own. Jan Lenica's award-winning animated efforts (including an adaptation of Eugene Ionesco's *Rhinoceros*) made him one of Polanski's favorite filmmakers; his internationally acclaimed posters included Warsaw Opera productions, Andrzej Wajda films (*Kanal* and *Ashes and Diamonds*), and Polanski's first two features.

There were a number of the uncredited "extras" on the *Cul-de-Sac* crew, including a Mrs. Bill, who provided first aid. "I'm sure that's a lady who lived on Holy Island, an ex-nurse we got hold of, that if anything happened we could call on her to come on the set to repair any damage to any human being,"[32] said Roger Simons.

All told Polanski had a solid crew of vast experience backing him on his third feature film, men and women who had worked with many top-flight directors on some of the best films made in the UK. "These were pretty good staff British technicians who did the major features in this country,"[33] noted Simons.

Yet there were days when Polanski was convinced the entire crew, "everybody was against me, when I felt totally solitary in my work. Even with Gil [Taylor] it was difficult on Holy Island, it was not the same Gil I had on *Repulsion*. And I was a bit sad about it. I don't think they followed me the way they did on *Repulsion*. I don't think they understood the originality of the film, that they understood the concept of it."[34]

Despite his admiration for the director, Simons felt Polanski had only himself to blame for the lack of support he sometimes got from the crew. "Roman would admit to this day he's difficult to work with, he knows he is. . . . If Gene Gutowski said, 'We've done a deal with a crew, they're on eight-hour days, and we have to break for lunch at one o'clock,' Roman wouldn't give a toss about that, he wouldn't care one iota about what the deal was. He doesn't like to get up in the morning, that was the other problem. I have a crew sitting there at nine o'clock in the morning, and no director. And then he'd arrive and do his own thing. At eight o'clock at night when the crew want to have their dinner, he wants to carry on. They all say to me, 'Hold on a minute. We waited for two hours doing nothing, then he wants us to work into our dinner break.'"

"Roman does what Roman wants to do," said Simons, recalling a sequence where the crew blew up the chicken house. Further hindering "the most difficult sequence of all" was the fact that it was a night shot. Simons knew if they worked past midnight, they would lose the next day's shooting, "because the crew—they were on very little money—wouldn't have stood for working past midnight. But

Roman was going to get the shots that he wanted regardless of what I said or the crew wanted."

"I have this wonderful vision of getting all the petrol gel on the chicken house going, and Roman having an argument with Donald Pleasence or Lionel Stander. It was about half past eleven and we still hadn't blown up the chicken house. There was Michael Klinger, Bob Sterne, Gene Gutowski all disappearing, when they saw Roman saying to me, 'I want more time to do the shot.' Walking away because they didn't want to get involved with Roman. It wasn't about money, the crew wasn't going to work the next day, that was the deal. But we did go past midnight, we did shoot it, and we did come back the next day."[35]

FROM SCRIPT TO SCREEN

Roman Polanski and Gérard Brach desired only "to create a movie that would reflect our taste in cinema" when they set out to write the film they eventually called *Cul-de-Sac*. "We didn't want a clichéd thriller,"[1] said the director. Unlike *Knife in the Water*, a psychological drama he wrote to take advantage of a landscape he was impassioned with, the duo "had no design or any definite idea what we would be writing about," he recalled. They decided to set down "the kind of emotions, the kind of feelings, characters, atmosphere we'd like to see in a film." The result: "a study of human behavior and how people in very special circumstances react to each other."[2]

The first major directorial improvement on the written word comes minutes into the film as Richard sees Teresa and her paramour, Christopher, lying in the sand together. The third page of the script has her "in a bathing dress" with him lying on top of her and kissing her. The film, however, is far more provocative; Teresa is lying on top of him, bare-breasted, clad only in a pair of jeans. It's immediately obvious they're lovers.

The picture was originally titled *Riri*, the French equivalent of Dickie (Richard)—the gangster played by Lionel Stander. During the writing process it became *If Katelbach Comes . . .*, and then simply *Katelbach*. The name of the film was in a state of flux when it went into preproduction.

"I recall that the script was still in development when Voytek joined the team and had not yet got its final title," said the production designer's wife, Fionnuala Kenny. "Polanski was explaining to

Voytek that [it] needed to be a place from which a person could not escape, a sort of hell. Voytek came up with the phrase 'Terminal Island' and apparently Polanski laughed and said 'Yes, more or less, but not so sinister, more mundane—as terror often is.'"[3]

The extant shooting script in Polanski's archive appears to be the final draft, close to the start of filming. The title page supports Kenny's contention:

"KATELBACH"
Original Screenplay
by
ROMAN POLANSKI and GERARD BRACH
Translated by
John Sutro

The shooting script is remarkably close to the film, though it bears no date; it is not, however, without numerous differences. The dialogue as rendered by John Sutro—a producer acquaintance of Polanski's, not a professional translator—has been rephrased throughout the final film, but the intent is the same in almost every instance. There appears to have been little wholesale improvisation. (The director's archival script is identical to the copy housed in the British Film Institute, though the latter has revisions written in an unknown hand).

One notable alteration was made to accommodate the casting of Françoise Dorléac just days before shooting started. When Richard questioned George about Teresa's nationality, the scripted response was "My wife is American."[4] When the cameras rolled the line became "My wife is French." Coincidentally, George's car also switches nationalities—it's a French Citroën in the script, a British Jaguar in the film.

George and Teresa's kitchen conversation about the shrimp she didn't catch when she was out "shrimping" or rather dallying with her illicit lover—as George well knows but tolerates—is more abrupt and to the point in the film. Another conversation that takes place in the kitchen while George cooks his omelet and Teresa varnishes her nails appears in the script but not in the picture. This scene was apparently filmed and deleted in the editing stage:

GEORGE

You don't seem to care any more about your animals. . . . What are we going to do with all these hens if you've lost interest?

TERESA

Stuff an eiderdown.

GEORGE

You see, you couldn't care less.

TERESA

They're stupid.

GEORGE

God knows you wanted your chicken run badly enough.

TERESA

They make me sick. . . . Don't you think they're stupid?

GEORGE

And how. I've said so a dozen times.

TERESA

What do you know about it anyhow?[5]

The omelet scene itself makes a noteworthy departure from the script. There's no mention of George trying to juggle the eggs for his omelet, only to have one crash to the floor and a second break in his hand. The scene was seemingly improvised on the set by Donald Pleasence.

"Egg comedy" was an old familiar bit of business, an endless source of humor for silent and early sound comedians—as Roscoe "Fatty" Arbuckle demonstrated by juggling an egg and bouncing it off the floor while making an omelet in *The Cook* (1918). "In vaudeville, the egg was an ideal prop for jugglers, magicians and comedians," noted film historian Anthony Balducci. "An egg, which could so easily break and create a mess, offered suspense and comedy to a vaudeville crowd."[6]

The scene wherein Teresa applies lipstick and mascara to George's face—after playfully dressing him in one of her nighties—was suggested by an incident involving Polanski's first wife and their producer friend Pierre Roustang, on whom George was modeled. The three were sitting in a restaurant one day when "she started retouching her makeup," the director recalled. "Roustang, who was sitting beside her, watched the process with an appreciative eye. On impulse Barbara turned and playfully applied some lipstick to his mouth. The result so tickled her that she improved on it with some eye shadow. Slowly but surely she made him up as a woman. . . . The effect was startling and disturbing."[7]

The sequence Pleasence would recall as "the notorious nightgown scene,"[8] unarguably one of the film's highlights, was filmed more or less according to the screenplay. The scene is more inspired in performance under Polanski's direction than might be imagined by a mere reading of the script. Dorléac is especially animated, giggling uncontrollably in marked contrast to her bored and unamused demeanor for much of the film; Pleasence also makes the most of it, laughing maniacally.

The actor maintained Teresa "was really rather fond of George— that in fact on occasions they had quite a good time in bed together. We tried to bring this out, Françoise and I," despite Polanski's interpretation to the contrary. The bedroom scene was "a very difficult scene indeed to motivate. Why does he let her do it? He does so because they used to enjoy considerable love and sex games together—kinky games," the actor asserted. "In actual fact, both at the end of this scene and at the end of the one in the kitchen, she and George went into a genuinely loving embrace, but these were cut out in each instance. Even so, I think this feeling comes out, with or without directorial permission!"[9]

Tellingly, the bedroom scene was filmed on a Monday, July 5, after two days off, with the actors evidently well rested. The one notable unscripted element is the addition of soft jazz emanating from the portable radio. The day's meticulously detailed call sheet fails to indicate all the props, including the exercise machine and the wig Pleasence tried on in a deleted bit, as seen on a British lobby card. Neither the exerciser nor the hairpiece is mentioned in the script, suggesting on-the-set, in-the-moment inspiration.

The actors were encouraged to improvise when it came to dialogue, owing to the difficulties presented by the screenplay. "I rewrote most of my part, the dialogue, so that it fit the character," asserted Lionel Stander. "Polanski didn't speak very good English then. He let me say anything I wanted to say; there was no quarrel about that."[10]

In the scene where George tells Richard he'll have to consult an almanac to find out when the tide goes down, the script has Richard exclaiming, "One has to be sick in the head to live in a hole like this."[11] In the film he says, "You gotta be out of your skull to live in a hole like that." Later, Richard has George shave him with a straight razor—recalling the scene where the slave (Polanski) shaves his master (Andrzej Katelbach) in *The Fat and the Lean*. The burly Richard declines the electric alternative, explaining, "It tears my flesh."[12] In

Dorléac and Pleasence in a deleted scene (or test shot?) from Cul-de-Sac.
SIGMA III/PHOTOFEST

the film he adds, "I have delicate skin," heightening the humor of the situation.

"We all rewrote parts of our scripts," said Pleasence. "It wasn't that Roman didn't have a good grasp of the language or anything—I think he understood everything that was going on, always—but it was poorly translated from the French original that he'd written with Gérard Brach."[13] Gene Gutowski added, "Brach does mostly physical writing; the scripts are more adaptations than translations of his originals."[14]

Jack MacGowran found himself drowning in an abundance of words in John Sutro's translation when he shot the causeway scene, where he's trapped in his stranded car as the tide continues rising around it. "We came to a long passage and Polanski said, 'Don't mind what's written on the paper, say anything you like here, Jack.'"[15]

The director treasured the spontaneity of the moment for years to come. "He's sitting in the water . . . partly conscious and almost hallucinating," remembered Polanski. "I told him I wanted him to give some signs of it and he came up with this line. He was shouting, 'Richard, Richard . . .' and then suddenly a line escaped from his throat—'I've got a problem here!' Which I left in the film, of course."[16] Recalled MacGowran: "I didn't have to go into a long speech that was written down. And he was so delighted with it."[17]

At times the dialogue may well have defeated the actors. It is not hard to imagine Dorléac having difficulty with a monologue during the grave-digging sequence, where the script has Teresa outlining her recipe for homemade vodka, in meticulous detail. In the film she simply tells Richard, "It's pure medicinal alcohol,"[18] and leaves it at that—though the speech may have been shot as written and later scrapped.

The shooting script has Richard telling Katelbach they're in Cornwall when he finally gets him on the telephone. As George clarifies for him: "Quo Vadis, Penruddock near Lands End."[19] In the film, when Richard asks George where he is it's "Rob Roy, Lindisfarne Island, Northumberland." The change would seem to indicate the Holy Island location had yet to be found when the screenplay was written.

The castle in the script is named for *Quo Vadis*, the novel about Nero's Rome first published in 1895. The author, Henryk Sienkiewicz, was a beloved Polish poet who would've been well known to Polanski and Brach as well; the French edition of the novel was so popular it reportedly outsold the work of Émile Zola. In a deleted scene that was to have taken place in the turret, George's friends, the Fairweathers, seem to recall a movie version of *Quo Vadis*, apparently confusing it with *Ben-Hur*.

In the film, the castle takes its name from *Rob Roy* (1817) by Sir Walter Scott, who allegedly "wrote the whole thing there." Given the geographical location of the fortress in Northumberland, the switch makes much more sense. When Richard asks George how old the castle is he calls home, he says "1910" in the script. In the film, it becomes "11th century." Lindisfarne Castle was actually built by the English in 1550 to defend the harbor against Scotland and converted to an Edwardian country home at the turn of the 20th century.

Another aspect of the screenplay was reworked owing to local history and geography as well. In the script, the stained-glass window destroyed by the boy's rifle blast is identified as one designed by Czech Art Nouveau artist Alphonse Mucha. In the film it becomes a St. Cuthbert window, referring to the 7th-century monk who became Bishop of Lindisfarne. (The window was not original to the castle and was created and installed by the crew.)

George refers to the bratty child as Horace in the script and Marion Fairweather, the boy's mother, corrects him—it's Nicholas. The film reverses the faux pas; George calls him Nicholas, and Marion calls him Horace. The actor in question, Trevor Delaney, is identified as Horace in the film's end credits but Nicholas in the original British and French press materials.

When Teresa finds the boy has scratched her Thelonius Monk record she gives his ear a vicious pull. In the script he screams, "That Yankee bitch pulled my ear off!"[20] In the film the line has been changed to "froggy bitch" owing to the last-minute casting of Dorléac (who "was beside herself and bought me a fishing rod," said Delaney, to apologize for the scripted abuse that resulted in a "red raw" ear).[21]

Richard tells Teresa, "I don't dig birds like you,"[22] when she sneaks out of the house to chat with him during the scripted grave-digging scene; the line becomes "I don't dig chicks like you" in the film (inexplicably, it remains "birds" in the published screenplay). The term resurfaces in the script when the Fairweathers, their friend Cecil, and his apparent girlfriend Jacqueline, obviously unwelcome, prepare to depart after Marion has remarked that marriage does not suit George.

MARION

It was bound to end like this. He has gone completely off his rocker because of that bird.

GEORGE

Say that again.

MARION

One has only to look at "her" and see your horns.

GEORGE

That "bird" happens to be my wife. As for the cuckold he asks you to get the hell out of here and never come back.[23]

The dialogue is considerably sharper in the film, wherein "bird" is replaced by "tart," with George responding:

GEORGE

That "tart" as you call her happens to be my wife. Now take your bloody filthy insinuations and get the hell out of my . . . my . . . fortress. Out, get out!

George jumps on Richard's back after Richard attacks Teresa with his belt, in retaliation for giving him a hotfoot—a detail not used in the film. Teresa's explanation to George is also more dramatic in the script:

TERESA

He jumped on top of me and tried to kiss me. He said dreadful things . . . that I needed a real man who would do it to me as it should be done.[24]

In the film this has been atypically watered down:

TERESA
He tried to kiss me. He said dreadful things . . . that I needed a
real man, like him!

After George kills Richard, Teresa urges him to hurry; they must
flee before the tide comes and go to the police. As a car suddenly
approaches, the script makes it obvious he's expecting his antagonist's associates. "He stops, legs apart, unintentionally taking up the
stance of a cowboy ready for a brawl."

GEORGE
KATELBACH . . . I killed him . . . come on . . . run me down
. . . come out . . . come out . . . murderers . . . cowards . . . the
whole pack of you against one man.[25]

The film is nearly identical, except that George doesn't name
Richard's enigmatic boss. Just whom he anticipates is not quite clear,
but he's surprised when Cecil steps from the vehicle and announces
he's returned for his rifle. George is not laughing in the script as
he is in the film, as he calls for Teresa after Cecil's arrival: "it's for
you."[26] In the script, he then hurls his paintings through the precious
stained-glass window of his studio; in the film he smashes the can-
vases against the wall and sweeps the painting supplies off the table.

When George climbs onto the rock and crouches in a fetal position at the end of the picture—a moment filmed exactly as written—
he cries out for his first wife, Agnes. The reference is clarified in the
original British pressbook and in press releases for the benefit of
media but is relatively subtle in the film; she's scarcely mentioned up
to this point.

There were apparently scenes scripted but never filmed because
Polanski simply ran out of time, according to Tony Klinger. "I

Pleasence in the final scene of Cul-de-Sac. COMPTON FILMS

remember when they'd fallen behind schedule and Roman simply ripped some pages out of the script and said, 'Now we're back on schedule.' But I don't remember what the scenes were. The other thing he did to get on schedule," asserted Klinger, "was do the entire last scene [of] Donald Pleasence running through the water's edge and waiting for the plane in one take, which was an amazing piece of filmmaking."[27]

WAITING FOR KATELBACH

When Michael Kinger and Tony Tenser asked Polanski for an explanation of *Cul-de-Sac*, he was up front about his inspiration for the script. He told them it was about a couple who lived by the sea, a rich man and his crazy, extravagant wife—and a wounded gangster who "falls into the house, where he holds them hostage overnight while waiting for his boss, Mr. Katelbach—who, like Godot, never comes."[28]

The film is "more Samuel Beckett than John Huston, and is reminiscent of the experiments with surrealism and the theatre of the absurd Polanski had tried in his student films,"[29] as writer James Greenberg has observed. "What Polanski created with *Cul-de-Sac*," stated writer David Thomson, "was a cinema of the absurd, delving into situations of humiliation, role-playing and betrayal, and evoking an unsettling atmosphere quite unlike anything else of the big screen."[30]

Beckett's *Waiting for Godot*, the play that inspired Polanski to a large degree, is perhaps the most influential drama of the 20th century. The plot is deceptively simple: Two men wait for a savior who fails to arrive, despite an appointment of which one of them is more or less certain. "Beckett used the fundamental fact that, in his own words to me, 'all theatre is waiting' to create . . . dramatic tension of an unusual kind,"[31] according to the playwright's authorized biographer, James Knowlson. The Polanski film could easily have been called *Waiting for Katelbach*, as Ivan Butler suggested.

The filmmaker's friend, Andrzej Katelbach, not only served as the model for one of the two gangsters but lent his name to their unseen boss. Polanski eschewed more direct references to Beckett though the shooting script reveals at least one was intended as an inside joke of sorts in Stander's first telephone scene:

> Hello . . . hello . . . I want Canterbury, yes Canterbury, the Becket [sic] Hotel. A personal call to Mr. Katelbach, no I don't know the number.[32]

Polanski apparently decided the gag (used twice in the script) was a little too on-the-nose and excised it. In the film, Richard asks for the "St. Cuthberry Arms Hotel" in "Maplethorpe-on-Sea."

A visual joke that seemingly has its roots in *Godot* turns up in the script when Richard takes off his belt to whip Teresa, after she mischievously ends his nap on the terrace with the hotfoot: "He runs after her. His trousers fall down over his calves and make him stumble forward."[33] Beckett used this old burlesque bit, so familiar from the films of Laurel and Hardy and others before them, in the play's finale—when Estragon takes off his belt to hang himself, his trousers fall down. Polanski sacrificed the gag in the film, apparently realizing the moment would not be nearly as menacing were it included. It was exactly the sort of sight gag so firmly rooted in the era of silent movie comedy to which the director would give free reign—and stellar execution—in *Dance of the Vampires*.

Beckett's shadow looms large over the filmmaker's early work. In the best of his short films, *The Fat and the Lean* (1961), Polanski himself costarred opposite nonactor Katelbach as the subservient half of a master-slave duo that suggested Pozzo and Lucky of *Godot*—with Lean dancing to entertain his superior, much like Lucky—as well as Hamm and Clov of Beckett's *Endgame*. The short film is evocative of both plays from the beginning. The director's absurdist short *Mammals* (1962) revolves around a similar pair in a snowscape, where they fight over who will pull the other on a sled, in a give-and-take reminiscent of *Godot*'s Estragon and Vladimir.

The day before *Knife in the Water* opened in Manhattan in 1963, following its showing at the New York Film Festival, Polanski told the media he was ready to tackle a film version of *Godot*. Through a spokesman he announced plans to make it in Paris with a French cast on a budget of $50,000, and noted he was ready "to start shooting within a week,"[34] if the rights could be cleared. Peter O'Toole had publicized similar intentions the year before, hoping to make a low-budget film version in the West of Ireland with Jack Mac-Gowran as Lucky and a screen adaptation by Tom Stoppard. Both announcements were premature; Beckett refused to permit either plan to proceed.

Polanski and Andrzej Katelbach in The Fat and The Lean. BRITISH FILM INSTITUTE

Cul-de-Sac is often called "Pinteresque" in testament to its affinity with the work of British playwright Harold Pinter, himself heavily influenced by Beckett. Theatre critic Irving Wardle characterized Pinter's trademark style as "comedy of menace,"[35] a description that perfectly fits *Cul-de-Sac*, with Lionel Stander rudely imposing himself on and terrorizing the inhabitants of the castle within moments of his arrival.

Donald Pleasence contributes substantially to the Pinter vibe of the film, thanks to the huge impact he created in the title role in *The Caretaker*. Moreover, as the actor once suggested, the more aggressive of Polanski's gangsters resembled one of the characters in Pinter's *The Dumb Waiter* (1960), a play the director was familiar with in which two hit men wait in a room for their boss, who—like Godot and Katelbach—never comes. ("But Katelbach exists," as Polanski reminded one interviewer. "They speak to him on the phone.")[36]

The influence of Beckett on both Polanski and Pinter cannot be overstated. Jack MacGowran, widely considered the Irish playwright's foremost interpreter during his lifetime, is a prime Beckett

Pleasence in The Guest, *the film version of Harold Pinter's* The Caretaker. JANUS FILMS

component in *Cul-de-Sac*. Happy Days, the Enniskillen International Beckett Festival in Northern Ireland, screened the film in 2015 to underscore the connection. (The similarity of MacGowran's character name in *Cul-de-Sac*—Albie—to playwright Edward Albee, another disciple of Beckett and card-carrying absurdist, was almost certainly no coincidence.)

Did Polanski cast MacGowran and Pleasence given their affiliations with playwrights who influenced him? "Not specifically because they had done things for Beckett or Pinter," he explained to author Joseph Gelmis. "It was because they were the kind of characters I was looking for to do the kind of scenes I had in mind. It was rather Pleasence and MacGowran than Peter O'Toole and Gregory Peck."[37]

As David Thomson observed, "Beckett's exploration of universal human experience through a pair of philosophical bums had great

MacGowran in Beginning to End, *his one-man anthology of Samuel Beckett's work.* PBS/KCET PUBLIC TELEVISION

influence on the young Polanski, as did the disturbing plays of his contemporary Pinter, with their theme of, yes, imposition, laced with menace and black humor. Although he would downplay it," the casting of Pleasence and MacGowran, noted Thomson, "suggests more than mere coincidence."[38]

Writer Paul Coates found affinities with both Beckett and Pinter as well. *Cul-de-Sac* has "greater proximity"[39] to *Endgame* than *Godot*, he asserted, in its reversal of the characters' dominant and dependent relationships; he was also reminded of the Pinter-scripted film, *The Servant* (1963). Critic Philip French felt "The wounded gangsters . . . are somewhat reminiscent of Goldberg and McCann in [Pinter's] *The Birthday Party*."[40]

Given the continual conversation about Beckett that ensued during Polanski and MacGowran's two collaborations, it is hardly surprising the actor would become the go-between for further talks between author and director about bringing *Waiting for Godot* to the screen. "We had several conversations about it at different times, but he [Beckett] always insisted it was not a good piece for film. Maybe he didn't believe it could be done. But I did, and I wanted to do it very faithfully,"[41] said Polanski. However, Beckett was adamant, as he told MacGowran in a letter: "As it stands it is simply not cinema material. And adaptation would destroy it. Please forgive me . . . and don't think of me as a purist bastard."[42]

More than two decades after Beckett's refusal, the filmmaker jumped at the opportunity to portray Lucky in a 1989 presentation of *En attendant Godot* for French public television. The broadcast, directed by Walter Asmus based on Beckett's own production at the Schiller-Theater in Berlin, gave Polanski the chance to play the character he had emulated in *The Fat and the Lean* early in his career. It was the same role in which he had "discovered" MacGowran on the London stage.

BEHIND THE SCENES

THE LOCATION

Polanski traveled far afield before finding the perfect locale to capture what he and Gérard Brach had envisioned for *Cul-de-Sac*. The opening pages of the shooting script described "a huge deserted beach" in low tide, in close proximity to "a sort of castle with a number of turrets, an unexpected and absurd sight . . . situated on a promontory."[1] The precise location was unspecified, unlike the original screenplay that called for "a remote house in Brittany cut off by high tides,"[2] as Gene Gutowski recalled.

Michael Klinger, with his tendency to do things in a frugal manner, contemplated a coproduction deal with Avala Film of Belgrade, the first postwar studio in what was then Yugoslavia. The company was not without a track record—Françoise Dorléac had recently starred opposite Omar Sharif in an Avala coproduction of *Genghis Khan*—but the director was against the idea. Every movie he'd ever seen with Yugoslavian participation was a flop. "Besides," he argued, "what about our characters stranded in a house cut off by the sea? Wasn't Klinger aware that the Mediterranean had no tide to speak of?"[3]

To pacify the backer, Polanski flew to the locale and met with government officials. He viewed every stretch of beach at several locations, failing to find the one prerequisite: the extreme rise and fall of the ocean called for in the script. As he knew at the outset, the picture could not be made in Yugoslavia. "We would have needed another script, another story, another concept altogether," he said. "And we didn't need the Mediterranean weather, we needed the contrary, something like what you have in the film now."[4]

St. Michael's Mount, a medieval priory situated atop an island off the coast of Cornwall, had the tides but lacked the sense of desolation Polanski desired. After a "haphazard survey" of the British coastline in a single-engine Beagle piloted by filmmaker Stanley Long, the director "decided on a more rational approach and consulted the Royal Geographic Society."[5] Production designer Voytek remembered the process of finding the location differently: "We only had very little time before we started shooting and [would have had to] scrub the film. I went to the Architectural Record Bureau and explained what we wanted, an island with a tidal road—and they found one."[6]

Accompanied by production manager Bob Sterne and cinematographer Gil Taylor, Polanski embarked on a reconnaissance trip, according to the director. When they flew over a patch of land situated off the coast of Northumberland some 70 miles south of Edinburgh, they knew they had found the ideal setting for the film. Holy Island, with its rocky outcrops and sand dunes, mud flats, salt marshes, shorebirds, and wildflowers, was a perfect fit—never mind its centuries of religious history, its reputation for being haunted by ghosts, or its popularity as a tourist destination. "We were absolutely stupefied by the landscape,"[7] said Polanski.

Fionnuala Kenny recalled, however, that Voytek and other crew members went location scouting by helicopter. "Something about Holy Island spoke to Voytek and he took aerial photographs to show to Polanski. Shooting on an island would be fraught with difficulty, and be expensive as everything would have to be transported there, but Voytek was determined. He met with Polanski and explained his vision and Polanski backed him, which he always appreciated, because a lesser man might have backed down and bowed to pressure to shoot on the mainland.

"In later years and taking no credit, but giving it to the lighting cameraman, Voytek would say that his instinct was right because the light on an island is unlike the light anywhere else, eerily incandescent because of the surrounding sea. Holy Island was just compact enough for this to be effective."

Decades later, Kenny saw Polanski's *The Ghost Writer* and "had the strangest sensation that Voytek had designed it. Of course he did not, but that air of brooding menace was identical, in large measure because of the light and the sea . . . Voytek's great gift as a designer was his ability to find a visual metaphor for the script or play he was working on. Not so much a place, often, as a state of mind."[8]

While the crew built the henhouse and the boat jetty, Lindisfarne Castle was the real thing. The 16th-century structure, crowning the island, mandated adjustments in the script but was an inspired piece of casting for George and Teresa's abode. "Everything to do with it was something filmic, it was almost made for a film location,"[9] recalled actor William Franklyn. "The castle is a strange place, which had everything we needed really. We used the furniture from the castle to dress the rooms,"[10] observed Voytek. Indeed, Polanski was surprised by the collection of furniture he found there, most of which he was able to use.

The producers donated £1500 to the National Trust for the use of the castle, plus an additional £500 for an extension when the film ran over schedule. The fees would eventually finance the installation of electricity, enabling proper heating for the first time.

Everything else the company needed to make a picture in a distinctly nonstudio environment was accomplished by booking the local Village Hall for the duration of filming. The building was partitioned into sections, serving as production office (which had one telephone), makeup, wardrobe, hairdressing, camera room, and equipment storage.

THE CAUSEWAY

The island is linked to the mainland by a causeway measuring some four kilometers (nearly two and one-half miles), cut off twice a day by the tides that flood the road for more than five hours at a time. The causeway was scripted for a crucial role in the film nonetheless. By the end of the first week, the daily schedule was added to the production call sheets. "DO NOT CROSS BETWEEN: 3:50 a.m. and 9:20 a.m., 4:27 p.m. and 9:57 p.m."[11] The Movement Order in Simons' possession clearly spelled out the rules: "Unit members are warned, if they have to cross the causeway connecting the island to the mainland, that they abide by the tide timetable and try not to 'beat the tide.'"

Gil Taylor (left, in knit cap) filming Lionel Stander on the causeway. COMPTON FILMS

Filming on the causeway in Cul-de-Sac, *from left: Roger Simons, Robin O'Donoghue, Ted Sturgis, Roman Polanski, Gil Taylor, Roy Ford, Geoff Seaholme, and unknown.* SIGMA III/PHOTOFEST

Gene Gutowski, who was producing a West End musical at the time, had frequent reason to leave the island. Timing his departures and arrivals to coincide with the tide table he would surreptitiously depart, typically on the weekend, to grab a night train to London. It was a tricky business: the water would quickly rush in and cover the causeway more than six feet deep. Racing the tide with his wife Judy on one occasion, "I lost and had to spend several cold, uncomfortable and dangerous hours perched on the roof of an old army truck," Gutowski recalled in his memoirs. "I believe that Roman, the cast and crew, were gleefully watching my predicament from the shore until somebody took pity and sent a rescue boat to get me and Judy off."[12]

Polanski may have drawn enjoyment from the producer's plight. Despite their partnership in Cadre Films Ltd., which they had recently formed at Gutowski's urging, the director's right-hand man was more than a little distracted by the musical; the show caused him to miss the reconnaissance trip and much of the filming.

Gutowski got his comeuppance one morning when the director angrily summoned him to the set. "You're the producer, are you not? . . . and you're responsible for everything on this picture, especially that I lose no time from filming?" Gutowski agreed, realizing he was being set up. "*So what are you going to do about this?*" Polanski demanded, "pointing dramatically to a large pile of cowshit on the grass and several more nearby. 'My actors cannot work sliding around in shit, so do something about it!'"[13]

Nobody was immune to the rules of the causeway, however, including Polanski. "He left the set in a temper one day," said sound camera operator Robin O'Donoghue. "He had a temper tantrum; he got in the Jeep and drove across the causeway and he got stuck. That tide comes in fast."[14]

THE WEATHER

Polanski agreed with virtually every member of the cast and crew on one point. "The weather was dreadful, constantly changing[15] . . . the light altered drastically every few minutes. Sudden storms and fast-changing cloud patterns played havoc with our daily schedules,"[16] he said. The situation was déjà vu for the director, reminiscent of what he encountered while filming *Knife in the Water* in the Mazury Lakes region of Poland, "forcing us to interrupt scenes, to start on new ones or revert to half-completed ones that would now match the light."[17]

The weather was the worst it had been in 20 years, according to the locals. "We were freezing all the time," recalled Donald Pleasence. "It was summer but I have no recollection of the sun ever coming out, though it is shining in the film most of the time. We would sit around all day waiting for the sun to come out for a few minutes.

We'd ask the local fishermen in the morning what the weather was going to be like, if the sun was going to shine. They'd look up and say, 'It'll get out,'" said the actor, mimicking the locals' thick Northumbrian accent.

"During breaks in shooting, Roman, Françoise and I would be huddled together, trying to keep warm," recalled Pleasence. "The North Sea has got to be one of the coldest bodies of water on this earth. Funny though, when I was a kid we'd be on camping vacations and such and we'd run and jump in—I get cold just thinking of that now."[18]

Gil Taylor had perhaps the biggest problem of anyone with the weather, being charged with photographing the picture. "The climate up there is unbelievable," he said of Holy Island. "We had a foot of snow. We had hail, we had rain pouring down on us, and I had to make the whole thing look like August. We had trouble with the tides the wrong time of the day. . . . There was always a problem somewhere to be solved."[19]

LODGING AND THE LOCALS

The film's location and its inherent problems would continue to linger in the consciousness of those involved for years. "The one thing that comes to mind is the sheer hardship of living on this island,"[20] said Gene Gutowski. The problematic causeway was in some respects an advantage. "We became very close as a team of people,"[21] observed Simons. But eventually, "Holy Island claustrophobia took its toll on everyone. We were far too exposed to each other's company,"[22] recalled Polanski, who told a group of college students, "Living was real hell. . . . it was total agony."[23]

The island was barely able to accommodate the movie's cast and crew. "Living conditions were harsh. We were living in little rented rooms over pubs and private homes," said Gutowski.

"Accommodations were primitive at best."[24] Polanski insisted on a trailer, which he parked in an isolated location by the cemetery. When the trailer proved overly attractive to earwigs, an infestation the director likened to a horror film, he rented the mead brewery manager's house.

Donald Pleasence caused commotion on his arrival, driving "a mammoth and opulent Lincoln, the like of which the locals had never seen,"[25] according to one account. "He did have a very large Lincoln car which he brought back from America," concurred his daughter, Angela Pleasence. "In those days it was quite a sight!"[26] Pleasence had a house on the island where he lived with his wife for the duration of filming, as did Lionel Stander and Jack MacGowran; coincidentally, Angela visited the location with Donald's first grandchild, a baby roughly the same age as Lionel's and Jack's young daughters.

Françoise Dorléac had a private room but not to be outdone by Pleasence's star trappings, "arrived with dozens of suitcases," said Gutowski, "for which I had to rent a truck at the airport and an extra room to hang it all out. During her entire stay on Holy Island, Françoise only wore a pair of jeans and the same old sweater."[27] In addition to her voluminous luggage—20 valises by Polanski's calculations—she also smuggled into the country her noisy pet Chihuahua Jaderane, from whom she was inseparable.

To the delight of the film's cast and crew, Holy Island's six pubs were unbound by drinking laws and remained open day and night, with no resident officer of the law to enforce the curfew effective elsewhere in Britain. "Normally the pubs used to close at eleven o'clock at night," noted Robin O'Donoghue. "Since the police had no access to the island after the tide came in, and there were no police on the island—the pubs would stay open."[28]

"They just kept their own hours. No policeman would dare to get on the island to prosecute them," said Gutowski, recounting the local story of a pair of constables who visited from the mainland and were forced to spend an icy winter night without shelter. "One of them died from being left out in the open, nobody would let him in."[29] Added Polanski: "Somehow, the glee with which the locals recounted this tale seemed psychologically consistent with their principal sport, which was to kill as many sitting ducks as possible with a single shot from a homemade cannon loaded with rusty nails."[30]

The island's inhabitants were "very strange in-bred fisherfolks . . . very insular people. The language they spoke had [traces] of Danish,"[31] noted Gutowski, whose estimate of their number at 300 to 400 was double Polanski's. The community, which consisted of mostly sheep farmers in addition to fishermen, "were isolated from the rest of the world and they had bred themselves to idiots," stated Polanski, who felt they "resented outsiders descending on them for longer than a day or two."[32] Gil Taylor agreed: "We weren't liked in some of these pubs. They hated us."[33]

However, Roger Simons did not remember any hostility toward the cast and crew. "The islanders basically made a lot of money out of us because we were staying in their homes, they were renting out their rooms to us; we were eating in their facilities there. We weren't disruptive," he said. "Because we shot the whole thing either on the beaches or on the causeway or in the castle—we never shot anything in the town itself—I can't see why there would be any problem with us whatsoever."[34]

According to Nick Lewis of the National Trust, "The islanders didn't generally like the film as it focused on the causeway and castle but didn't reference the village. I'm not sure they appreciate the explanation that Polanski was trying to emphasize the isolation of the building!"[35]

Despite their natural curiosity, the locals interfered only minimally with the filming. "Normally there's the problem [on location] of the general public watching us," said Simons. "I don't think on

Cul-de-Sac we had that problem. There might've been a few odd people about watching, certainly, but only a few. Roman wouldn't have had that, he likes a closed set."[36] There were several outsiders who visited the location, however, including fashion photographer David Bailey, a friend of the director.

THE FOOD

Lunch and dinner were provided for the company at three small hotels. Complaints about the food were rampant. "The islanders' staple dish was boiled mutton, and the crew conveyed their opinion of it in a ritual that steadily lost its entertainment value as the weeks went by: whenever they had boiled mutton for lunch, they returned to the set bleating like sheep,"[37] recalled Polanski.

"We seldom left the island, except to go to a restaurant on the mainland a few times," Donald Pleasence remembered. "But then it was difficult to get back, because of the tides. We ate a lot of salmon while we were up there, so we didn't starve."[38] On the other hand, they didn't exactly dine like visiting royalty. "The food was unbelievable. Everywhere in England the food is bad, but here it was inedible,"[39] Polanski groused years later.

"Tweed salmon [from the nearby town of Berwick-upon-Tweed] is supposed to be the best in the world, but the pub cooks stewed it till the flesh turned to gray mush, whereas the skin, by some mysterious process, became even tougher,"[40] the director noted in his memoirs. No sooner had he completed the film than he told the *New York Times*, "It's a sort of black comedy. And that place had the blackest, worst food I've ever eaten."[41]

The filmmaker, who was of the opinion the best salmon came from North America, asserted he had 150 pounds of the freshwater-bred fish flown to the location from the Stage Delicatessen in Manhattan. It may not have been an idle boast; the Seventh Avenue institution was highly regarded by its show business clientele, one of whom was among his cast. To combat the "horrible" reality of living on the island while making the picture, "I called Max Asnas of the Stage Delicatessen and ordered forty pounds of pastrami and some dry ice," said Lionel Stander. "They flew it to London and then from there it was flown to Berwick-upon-Tweed or someplace. They had a hard time getting it to us. We all feasted on that, then another time I had some steaks flown up from London."[42]

It was more like 20 pounds of pastrami according to Polanski, who likened Stander to his uncouth character in *Cul-de-Sac*, remembering him as "a loudmouth" and "a bully." The actor amused the company at first, and they lent a sympathetic ear to his accounts of the blacklist era. But "as the same old stories received their umpteenth airing, we tired of pastrami, Stander, and the sound of his raucous laugh."[43]

Stander apparently had problems with the island's liquid refreshment as well as the food. On one occasion he "knocked back a bottle of dynamite-strength local spirit and promptly went blind for a day," recounted author Christopher Sandford. The actor claimed several times he "wasn't long for this world."[44]

AFTER HOURS

Polanski had an intimate relationship with Jacqueline Bisset during the making of the film, or so he implied in his memoirs. He recalled her as one of his few "congenial companions . . . whose nature was as lovely as her looks" and remarked on her "consoling presence"[45] during the problematic shooting schedule. Bisset herself has described both the director and the film as "brilliant"[46] but has steadfastly refused to discuss or confirm their off-camera association in interviews.

"News to me," Roger Simons said on hearing of the alleged tryst. "It's entirely possible. . . . Knowing Roman it wouldn't surprise me, but I'm surprised I didn't know. It's highly probable Roman did have something going . . . I can't see Roman spending [nine] weeks on Holy Island not having sex. The chances are he did have a relationship with Jackie Bisset. It makes total sense now but I wasn't aware of it."[47]

Noted Tony Klinger: "I had no knowledge of Roman and her having any relationship but it wouldn't surprise me; well, it would a little, since I had always thought he strongly fancied Françoise Dorléac but I don't know if that was reciprocated."[48]

Bisset arrived the start of the fifth week according to the call sheets, remaining three weeks on location. "The chances are she'd have been there . . . as weather cover," said Simons. "We probably only shot with her for a few days. She was probably on stand-by—be available on the island to shoot interiors if the weather was bad."[49]

Actress Jill St. John, with whom Polanski had a casual affair during the making of *Repulsion*, visited the director on location. By the time she arrived, however, Bisset had fortunately completed her scenes and left Holy Island.

According to Simons, "there were a few relationships that went on" during the filming. "The one that I particularly remember which was the biggest drama of the whole lot was the one between Françoise Dorléac and the camera operator, Roy Ford. I don't think they could escape from being public, because of the fact that the island was so small."[50]

Dorléac, who had recently had an affair with François Truffaut, apparently made no attempt to hide her little fling with Ford. The actress was "bored and miserable" on location, said Polanski; she disliked her costars on sight and considered the locals "barbarians." Furthermore, she was "too quintessentially French to join in the pub-crawling that was our only after-hours relaxation," observed the director, who concurred that Dorléac "eventually found solace in the arms of Roy Ford . . . and became much more relaxed."[51]

Screening films became one of Polanski's chief pastimes in the evening, but it was work more so than pleasure. "Roman insisted on seeing rushes on a daily basis, and quite rightly so, just to make sure how we were doing," recalled Simons. "The problem was of course we had to get the film back to London to get processed. So we weren't getting the rushes back on a daily basis."[52]

Once the footage was processed, they had trouble viewing it: "We hired this movie theatre, a cinema in Berwick [about ten miles away], but then we couldn't get off the island to see them; we couldn't get back because of the tide. We then decided to get the Village Hall, which was our production office. We got a projector, and we got a projectionist sent up from London and ran our own rushes," said the assistant director.

The filmmaker did have at least one outlet for pure recreation. "Because we used to go in the evenings to the Village Hall, to watch the film after dinner, Roman started to build this electric train set," remembered Simons. "So we used to stay on after rushes—nothing else to do on Holy Island apart from go to bed—and we used to play with trains in the evening. We used to play games because there was nothing to do. I wasn't a drinker, Roman wasn't a drinker, so we often used to meet up in the evening."[53]

Polanski would occasionally visit the public houses to socialize with members of the crew. He particularly enjoyed the company of his editor, Alastair McIntyre, who livened up evening pub sessions on Holy Island with "a hilarious Scottish vocal act,"[54] as he recalled. He and McIntyre, with whom he would make six pictures, "were very close," said Simons. "Roman would spend most evenings with him, looking at rushes in the Village Hall. I don't know whether Alastair cut the film up there, or he came up to show rushes to Roman and then went back to London and cut at Twickenham."[55]

THE PERFECTIONIST

"Roman was very demanding," Robin O'Donoghue said pointedly. "He wanted it correct; he wanted it his way. I don't remember him compromising. They're in the castle, Donald Pleasence opens the fridge to get something out—when you open the fridge and you breathe out, in real life, you get a mist, you get condensation from your breath. Roman wanted that. I think they put smoke in his mouth so when he opened the fridge—it looked real, it looked like condensation 'cause the fridge was so cold."[56]

On a morning he was preparing to film an interior scene, Polanski was walking the set. "There was a kitchen table on the set, with the drawer turned away from the camera," recalled Voytek's wife, Fionnuala Kenny. "Without pausing in his stride, Polanski said, 'What's in the drawer?' Voytek didn't dress the set, so he didn't actually know, but he knew he could not say that so he took a wild guess. 'Knives,' he said. Polanski pulled the drawer open. Inside were three symmetrical Sabatier knives. Polanski smiled and moved on. [Art director] George Lack laughed and everyone breathed a sigh of relief."[57]

"I remember Roman was a stickler for authenticity," recalled Trevor Delaney. "The scene with the shotgun where I shoot the pane glass window out he wanted live ammo in the gun. Apparently the crew threatened to go on strike so in the end blanks were used. Same with Robert Dorning—after the gun incident he smacks my backside. The crew wanted padding but Roman wanted it real and after umpteen takes I was crying. (My mum said he apologised and was very sorry.) Similarly with biting Donald Pleasence's finger—my turn to inflict pain—that take went on and on and in the end Donald had deep teeth marks in his finger."[58]

When a scene in *Repulsion* called for a door to be splattered with blood, prop man Alf Pegley had used a syringe filled with what the director called "my 'secret formula' for blood—cochineal and

Nescafé."[59] When the syringe failed to produce the desired effect, Gene Gutowski provided him with a bicycle pump. Pegley's services were again called on for *Cul-de-Sac*, but the "secret formula" was not, owing to "Roman's desire to have real blood and not fake blood," remembered Roger Simons.

"Roman got a coach driver and bought some chickens; he got the driver to kill the chickens, to use the blood on the actors. And that caused a lot of aggravation. A number of the crew were very upset at the blood that was being [used] on Lionel Stander when he got shot. There were huge problems about this fuss," said Simons.

"You do everything as if it's for real. You don't stand by the camera and watch the scene going on and think in black and white, you're absolutely thinking color although you're shooting in black and white." Stressed Simons: "Roman just feels, he wants everything to be authentic; he thought the makeup blood didn't look right. The other problem [was], the texture of the blood wasn't right."[60]

"I remember them doing a test 'cause it was black and white, what is the best thing to use for real blood," added O'Donoghue. "Roman checked it and checked it and checked it, what was the closest thing to real blood? He was into the details."[61] Similarly, there would be dissatisfaction over the color of the blood while filming the finale of *Chinatown*.

Polanski also strived for realism when it came to the sound, as with the movie's telephone conversations. "We had to rig up a practical telephone," said O'Donoghue. "We had to put another actor, most likely the continuity girl, Dee Vaughan, in another room [as the unseen telephone operator], so she could have a proper conversation with him [Lionel Stander], so you're not trying to put the pauses in yourself."[62]

Postproduction on the film was simplified to some extent by Polanski's directorial choices. "He didn't want to do dubbing," said O'Donoghue, who nonetheless recalled an instance that did require it. "One of the actors goes out on the terrace. Roman wanted a star-tled seagull, squawking and flying off. The sound editor was David Campling; he got a seagull squawk and put it in. Roman says, 'No, no, David, this is no good, get me another one.' David produced another one. 'No, no, I do it.' They put a microphone up. Roman made the seagull squawk he wanted, as it flew away."[63]

Lionel Stander was reportedly given to doing a mean-spirited impression of Polanski on occasion during the shoot. He was forced to concede, however, that the director was "a natural leader. . . . He'd shin up a cliff or jump in and stand half immersed in freezing cold water to get a shot. Roman never asked you to do anything that he didn't do himself. His impulse to active leadership and his instinct to always be on the attack were phenomenal, and it was a genuinely inspiring sight to see the little brat right there at the head of his troops."[64]

RETAKES AND POSTPRODUCTION

Postproduction on *Cul-de-Sac* took place at the venerable Twick-enham Film Studios, in Richmond upon Thames in South West London. While the director recalled shooting retakes at Shepperton Studios in Surrey, Roger Simons insisted, "There's no question it was Twickenham."[65] Robin O'Donoghue clarified, "Roman may have done some ADR [automated dialogue replacement, or looping] or post syncing" at Shepperton, he added. "It may have just been a little fix at the end."[66]

A single call sheet for Twickenham dated August 18, 1965, Polanski's 32nd birthday, is extant. Simons' recollection of at least one more day in the studio concurred with Pleasence's and Gutow-ski's memories of a key scene that had to be reshot. "Because of the pressures of time . . . after we left Holy Island, an outdoor terrace set had to be built in the studio, so that Donald Pleasence could kill Lionel Stander, this time properly,"[67] observed Gutowski.

Pleasence remembered the completion of the scene taking place two months after the company left Holy Island. "We had to come back to the studio, rebuild the terrace and shoot the murder again—for some reason we were unable to do it properly the first time," he recalled. "From the moment George comes out of the wine store [cellar] with the gun in his hand up to the killing of Richard, it was all done in the studio and later beautifully matched up with the location work."[68]

Polanski, who found himself "absolutely drained" by the experience of making the film, also needed some retakes on location despite Compton's resistance in returning to the scene of the crime. "After much fighting I got a little crew to go and shoot something. I can't remember the name of the director of photography because Gil [Taylor] wasn't available any more. But I had to show him the film. I remember he told me, 'The film is not good.'"[69]

The director was obliged to promote *Repulsion* while editing *Cul-de-Sac* but gave the latter his full attention beginning in mid-October 1965. "He watches over the editing as closely as over everything else, keeping a tighter hold than most people I've worked for," editor Alastair McIntyre reflected, "but this does not mean he never allows his editor any freedom of expression."[70] He clearly held the director in high esteem; as McIntyre told an interviewer, "His technical skills, his sense of what looks and sounds right, are absolutely uncanny. He's a very difficult chap, you know, very exacting and uncompromising, but it's worth it because Roman's quite a unique fellow."[71]

McIntyre was made aware how exacting Polanski could be. One day when they were mixing *Cul-de-Sac*, recalled Robin O'Donoghue, "Roman says to Alastair, that shot is too long. 'Take twelve frames off that shot.' So Alastair goes into the projection box and cuts it.

They run it again. And Roman says, 'No, no, now you've taken out fifteen frames.' Mac [McIntyre] has the trim in his pocket, he counts it out—fifteen frames."[72]

For all his attention to detail, the director preferred to be surprised when it came to Krzysztof Komeda's wonderfully weird score. "I didn't sit with him as he composed. He'd just come with something prepared," said Polanski. "I often didn't even attend recording sessions, because I wanted to hear the music with fresh ears when I finally heard it synced to the picture. I'd usually leave him with the editor and come back to see the final result."[73]

Polanski took a hiatus from cutting the film for a brief skiing vacation in Austria with Gene Gutowski, producer Andy Braunsberg, *Playboy* executive Victor Lownes, and other friends. Michael Klinger was upset with him and Gutowski for going AWOL, but they managed to enjoy themselves nonetheless. Postproduction continued through the rainy Christmas holiday season in 1965, with actors rerecording dialogue in a small studio in Paris.

The distress caused by the strain of filming the picture was relieved during postproduction not by the holidays or the skiing trip but by an LSD trip—a first-time experience for the director—at a time when the drug was legal. "While still hallucinating I'd grasped a peculiar fact," said Polanski. "There was nothing in my nightmarish visions about Holy Island, nothing about *Cul-de-Sac* and its attendant tribulations. My depression had gone. In some strange way, the acid had cured it."[74]

THE TROUBLE WITH ACTORS

"I've never had such bad working relationships with actors, and at the end of the shoot no one could stand each other,"[1] Roman Polanski told an interviewer shortly after completing *Cul-de-Sac*. "It is never long, during the making of any film, before the off-set atmosphere begins to reflect that of the story itself," he observed in his memoirs. "Unfortunately, our trio of principals soon started playing their parts for real."[2]

Polanski contemplated calling it quits as a director and returning to acting. "I really considered it seriously. It was no joke. I nearly had a breakdown, I was so disgusted by that experience," he told author Joseph Gelmis. "But what matters is that the film stands exactly as I wanted it to, and it's an addition to the poetic language of cinema. . . . I always believed in it. It is real cinema, done for cinema, like art for art."[3]

The film the director has most often cited as his favorite was born, conversely, of his least favorite experience. What might have seemed a relatively carefree situation in preproduction turned out to be anything but once the cameras rolled. "Let's be honest, this film should've been one of the easiest films ever to make," said assistant director Roger Simons. "There was basically a four-handed cast. One of them is in a car for most of the film or lying on a table half-dead. And so you discount him. You're dealing with a three-hander film with a very talented director, on a controlled location, in Holy Island, where there were no onlookers, no problems with the outside looking in; it should've been a very simple film to make, and it certainly wasn't.

"Jack MacGowran was a delight—the loveliest man you ever met—but there was no love lost between any of the [other] actors and Roman," asserted Simons. "Apart from the physical problem of making the film, we had a problem with Lionel Stander being a real pain in the ass. Donald Pleasence was not an easy man to work with, and Françoise Dorléac was a bit strange. And Roman [was] winding them up all the time. All the ingredients were there for a real difficult movie."[4]

Gil Taylor, whose striking cinematography greatly enhances the film, cited Polanski's rabid attention to actor and performance as one ingredient in the director's distinctive approach: "Roman's temperature on a set is never 98.6. It's usually about 106. He dominates actors. He breaks them down until he's made the exact character that he wants."[5]

Pleasence had the lead "yet seemed to want to upstage everyone else. He hogged the camera in a variety of ingenious ways," recalled Polanski, noting the actor "looked down on the rest of the cast and was subtly mean to them."[6] The trouble began on day one when Pleasence arrived with his head shaved, sans prior approval. "That was the guy we got, we couldn't change this so shaven he was. It seems to me now a good idea," the director said in hindsight. "Although this lent his performance an extra twist, I was annoyed that he hadn't consulted me first."[7]

Though Pleasence considered *Cul-de-Sac* one of his favorite film performances, he readily admitted actor and director were not always in sync. "I think that was Polanski's best picture. We were very creative together and although we had fights, a lot of the scenes were improvised on the spot,"[8] he stated.

The relationship between George and Teresa was one aspect of the film where the actor did not see eye to eye with Polanski. "He fell flat on his face for her—something strange and exotic in his dull world. She went for his money, of course, but she liked him as well," said Pleasence. "This was an area where Roman and I disagreed. He was absolutely adamant that she did not find George attractive in any way. This was the only thing that bothered me, at least as far as the development of character was concerned."[9]

Polanski and his male lead disagreed on other facets of the character, according to Stander. "Pleasence didn't want to wear the nightgown, he was afraid of hurting his image or something. After the third day of shooting, he and Roman weren't talking."[10] Said Simons: "I wouldn't be surprised. But obviously there was conversation; Roman would never have gotten that performance out of Donald if they weren't speaking. I think Donald had a respect for Roman as a director. But Roman is not easy to work with and is very demanding; any actor would have respect and yet concern about the way Roman directs."[11]

Stander further asserted, "Pleasence's wife [Josephine] caused a lot of the trouble."[12] Reflected Simons, "I remember Donald's wife having conversations with Roman. I don't remember ever seeing her on the set; if anything like that happened it would've been behind the scenes at the end of the day. Generally, working on a Polanski film is different from working on any other film and Donald would've been very aware of that. He would've tried to get his way with Roman, and Roman would certainly do the reverse and get his way with Donald. There's a natural actor-director animosity there before you start."[13]

Following the shoot, the actor found himself frequently asked the same question about his director: "Was he nice?" "Not especially. At least not to me," Pleasence told one interviewer. "But yes, as he prowled round the set, it was clear that he knew most of the crew personally, and what's more, understood their jobs: which lens to use and how exactly a certain light would look. It's a rarer skill in directors than you'd think. But then he'd abruptly bollock Stander or me, and the whole thing would come to a halt," recalled the actor. "So, on balance, Roman wasn't nice. He was an average, Hollywood-type megalomaniac, an unsentimental, restless young man. He was also about twenty IQ points brighter than most directors. You were always conscious of being in the hands of an absolute master of his trade."[14]

Pleasence was philosophical about his disagreements with the director, observing, "Out of this, I think, came something very exciting."[15] His daughter acknowledged the conflict. "Yes, it was a difficult working relationship with Polanski, but then, I think most of the actors had a similar time," reflected Angela Pleasence. "In those days Polanski was not the easiest. But . . . the film is stunning. What more can one say?"[16]

"Donald was a complicated man," said Simons. "I liked Donald; I did three films with him. But he didn't get on greatly with Lionel." The assistant director fondly recalled how Polanski captured a little of that behind-the-scenes antagonism on film, by wiring the actors together for the scene near the end of the picture where Pleasence kills Stander. "Because neither Donald or Lionel liked each other very much and Roman loved the fact, he kept them wired up together all day long. They had to go to the loo together and everything.

"If I remember rightly, Donald fires the gun, and Lionel goes down . . . one of the shots causes the chicken house to blow up. We spent a day rehearsing. Roman didn't want to do a shot of the gun firing and the bullet [hitting]. He didn't want to do them in separate shots; he wanted to see the gun and the hit in the same shot. We rigged it so there's a wire that goes from the gun, up Donald's shoulder, down his trouser leg, and up Lionel's trouser leg [to where] the bullet hit . . . and so Roman kept them together with this wire all day long,"[17] said Simons, who laughed at the memory.

Polanski had even greater difficulties with Stander than he did with Pleasence. The former's "inordinate resemblance" to his abrasive movie persona was only the beginning, noted the director, who

Lionel Stander and Donald Pleasence were at odds with each other on and off screen. SIGMA III

found the actor's "almost manic enthusiasm" for his work soon dissipated. Whenever Polanski gave the actor feedback on his performance, "he would enumerate the reasons underlying his decision to move or speak in a certain way," said the filmmaker. "He construed all my suggestions as an affront, assuming them to be motivated by hostility toward him as a person or disdain for him as an actor."[18]

Stander, who was friendly only with MacGowran among the cast, recalled the contretemps differently. "Polanski never had any problems with me about interpretation or the character," he stated. "The only problem we had was a scene where I had to throw the corpse into a grave, and we shot it maybe 35 times. [Writer] Gérard Brach was doubling for Jack—he was all wrapped up in the burlap—and I had to carry him, and then throw him into the ground. I got a hernia doing it. And I tried to suggest to Roman that he shoot it a different way, and he wouldn't listen. He said, 'Lionel, I'm the director. Don't argue.'"[19]

According to one of Polanski's biographers, Stander was vexed when he viewed the rushes of the scene with the director and realized only his feet were visible on the screen. "I don't mind getting a hernia, but I'd like the audience to see me getting it,"[20] he reportedly complained to the director. "He told me he got a hernia, but I thought he said it was from pushing the car in the opening scene," recalled his daughter, Bella Stander.[21] The actor also claimed he wrenched his knee and began to limp "theatrically," according to Polanski. Michael Klinger was convinced Stander's intent was "to spin out the shooting for as long as possible because his contract entitled him to extra fees if we overran a certain date,"[22] noted the director, though Klinger later hired him to appear in *Pulp*.

"Polanski wasn't always easy to work with, but I could see he had a good idea for the picture, and it was one of the biggest parts I ever played," Stander said in retrospect. "It is one of my favorite of all my roles."[23]

The actor's behavior was "truly impossible" during the filming, Polanski contended. "He started to become extremely lazy. Good living and good booze were much more interesting to him than the work."[24] Stander was also "quite nasty" to Dorléac, taking out his hostility on the actress after she awakened his screen character by giving him a hotfoot. When he whipped her with the belt, he did it for real with the belt buckle on at least one take. Then he began screaming, claiming she had caused injury to his knee. "He was very difficult," stated Polanski, "but . . . that was the role we asked him to play. We wanted him to be like that, there was a lot of it in Lionel and we were getting it out of him twelve hours a day, so no wonder that he was like this."[25]

In addition, Stander had a history of heart trouble he neglected to tell insurance underwriters about during preproduction. "He'd had at least one heart attack already, in 1962," recalled Bella Stander. "I would imagine he didn't mention it as he'd just come off the blacklist.

This was his biggest role ever. He'd never had such a major role, a part where he wasn't just the sidekick. *Cul-de-Sac* was a big break for him."[26]

When Stander began complaining of chest pains and visited the Royal Victoria Infirmary in Newcastle for tests—which proved negative—the insurance company threatened to terminate their participation. They backed off only with the promise he would work no more than six hours on any given day. "It became catastrophic,"[27] reported Polanski, until Gérard Brach, with whom Stander would socialize after hours, spread a rumor the director wanted to star him in his next film but was reconsidering the idea.

The project, *Chercher la Femme*, had been commissioned by Pierre Roustang prior to *Repulsion*. The romantic comedy would be discussed with Tony Curtis after *Cul-de-Sac* was completed but never made, despite a three-picture deal with Compton; it more than served its purpose, however. Stander had only to hear that "I started having second thoughts," said Polanski, and he fell for the ruse. "Strange as it seems, it worked perfectly, and again he became completely manageable. . . . Miraculously Stander's knee and chest pains vanished. Throughout our last couple of weeks on Holy Island his behavior was impeccable."[28]

In retrospect, the filmmakers should not have been too surprised by working with Stander. He had, after all, given them a sneak preview. "Lionel was a bit of an animal," observed Roger Simons. "The day before shooting [began] we had a cocktail party. Everybody had a drink together. Lionel decided he ought to show the crew what he was like. I remember him eating raw eggs. That was our opening; the first thing he did was prove he was a man by eating raw eggs. We thought, we've got twelve weeks of this to come."[29]

Where Angela Pleasence declined to comment on Polanski's remarks about her father in his memoirs, Bella Stander was happy to address the director's statements regarding her dad. "'No one else could get a word in.' That's true. 'A compulsive talker who had to be the center of attention at all times.' That's true. 'We began by eating his pastrami, laughing at his jokes, and providing him with the court he needed.' That's him all over. Him calling Françoise Dorléac a 'stupid cunt?' I don't doubt it at all."

There was another side to Stander that few people ever saw, though. "His public persona was a brave, brash guy," said Bella. "When he was by himself he was quiet and read all the time. All. The. Time. He read a book a day. When I visited him in Rome [at a later date] he was so bored he was reading the dictionary." [30]

Having appeared as a spoons player in a street band in *Repulsion*, Polanski made an even more fleeting cameo in *Cul-de-Sac*. During retakes at Twickenham Film Studios the director required an insert of "a hand smacking Françoise Dorléac," recalled Simons, "and I remember Roman said, 'It has to be me doing it.'"

The hand ostensibly belonged to Lionel Stander, but "It had to be Roman's hand that did it,"[31] said Simons. For Polanski, much as it had to be him who appeared to strike Dorléac, it would have to be him who sliced open Jack Nicholson's nose in *Chinatown*—but unlike the affectionate rapport between Jack and Roman, there was seemingly no love lost between Françoise and her director.

However, Robin O'Donoghue dismissed the notion that Polanski was abusive in his treatment of Dorléac at any time. "I never saw anything on *Repulsion* or *Cul-de-Sac* to suggest that Roman was anything but a passionate, caring film maker. I never saw any bullying towards Françoise but he would fight to get what he wanted," said the sound camera operator, insisting the director shot the insert "because he knew how it would cut together, not so he could slap her. When actors hit or slap each other it is what we call 'pulled.' It's a slap but controlled, it doesn't hurt. In postproduction we add the sound of a real slap or punch which makes it seem real."[32]

The incident with the hand summed up the working relationship between actress and filmmaker in Simons' view. If Polanski found directing Catherine Deneuve in *Repulsion* "like dancing a tango with a superlatively skillful partner,"[33] working with her older sister proved much less satisfactory. Dorléac "felt that Polanski's treatment of her was manipulative, as if she were an object," according to Polanski biographer Barbara Leaming. "Although she was eventually satisfied with the film, she complained bitterly about Polanski's problems communicating with women."[34]

Donald Pleasence felt one aspect of the actress's difficulties was a disagreement over her role, not unlike his own contretemps with the director. "Teresa is not just a girl who marries a man for his money and then gets very bored and fed up," said the actor. "Of course she *is* bored, but Françoise wanted the character to be more two-dimensional, whereas Roman wanted her to be simply sluttish. I don't think he ever really liked her performance very much, though I myself thought it was great."[35] Dorléac was in agreement: "I didn't like the character of the girl I played at all. She was so egotistic, so self-centered, never thinking of anyone but herself."[36] Observed Simons, "She was very young, and Roman treated her like Roman treats ladies . . . their relationship was very hot in terms of director and leading lady. She was working with knowing his relationship with Lionel and Donald wasn't easy, so she was in the middle of all that. Roman is very much the boss, he's in conflict with most people all of the time."[37]

The discord was exacerbated when Dorléac lost a filling and flew to Paris, trusting the care of her teeth only to French dentists despite the disruption it caused in the schedule. Unfortunately, she took her pet Chihuahua with her, hiding it in her handbag when she flew back to England. Gene Gutowski came to her rescue when the dog bit a customs official at Heathrow airport, "but it took all his fixer's finesse to sort things out; breaking the British quarantine relations

Françoise Dorléac and her best friend, Jaderane.
COMPTON FILMS

was a serious offense," recalled Polanski. "The Chihuahua was flown back to Paris, making Françoise more miserable than ever."[38]

Iain Quarrier found himself at odds with his director friend when he couldn't do the one thing requested of him for his small role as Dorléac's paramour. Though he had weeks to learn to walk on his hands, he barely managed two or three steps when it came time to shoot the scene. Polanski nonetheless would give his French-Canadian pal a featured part in *Dance of the Vampires*. "Iain was quite a character and a great mate of Roman's," recalled Ferdy Mayne, his costar in the latter film. "He and Roman just lit up the soundstage with their enthusiasm. But make no mistake, Iain was a party animal and as decadent as the era would allow."[39]

Iain Quarrier tries to make a good impression on Polanski, in a scene from
Dance of the Vampires. METRO-GOLDWYN-MAYER STUDIOS/ALAMY

The neophyte actor also had a falling-out with cinematographer
Gil Taylor during *Cul-de-Sac*. "I liked Iain very much. It's strange to
say. I did like him; we were very friendly . . . but I think something
happened to him, I think he used to take a little dope here and there,"
asserted Taylor, who described an unpleasant encounter with Quarrier
at a party thrown by Donald Pleasence: The veteran cameraman, who
was 51 at the time, was dancing with his wife-to-be, script supervisor
Dee Vaughan, who was more than 20 years younger and "was looking absolutely gorgeous," in Taylor's words. Quarrier began making
impolite remarks until Taylor felt compelled to act. "He was standing
against a low wall and there was a drop of about 10 feet. I said, 'Actors
don't pass remarks like that to mature people like me. 'Cause if you
do . . .' I gave him a right upper cut, and he went right over. Roman
said, 'Why did you hit Iain?' I said, 'He talks too much after dark.' So
he [Polanski] said, 'Good thing. Does him a lot of good.'"[40]

Jack MacGowran was the one performer Polanski enjoyed a close relationship with on *Cul-de-Sac*. "First of all, working with him, I realized how exciting an actor he was. What he was doing was so funny—so right—on top of everything he was so easy to work with," stressed the director. "Jack was all like butter; I'd say, 'Do this way, do that way,' he would do it."

Apart from Gérard Brach, Polanski found MacGowran was "the only person I could really talk to" on Holy Island. "Also he was an extremely patient actor; he would never complain. When you set up the shot and lay him on the table as a corpse, in some sort of rigor mortis contortion, he would lay there until you said 'Stop,' because often you forget, you go to lighting, to other departments and he's laying there stiff, without moving, without budging."[41]

MacGowran had never been enamored of making pictures up to this point in his stage-driven career. "After I met Polanski my whole idea of the cinema changed," said the actor, who defended the number of takes he was inclined to shoot. "Where another director will say, 'That'll do for me,' Roman will want to try once, twice or a dozen times more and such is the infectious quality of his enthusiasm that whereas with another director I might well have walked off the set, here I was able to keep going through all forty of them."[42]

The filmmaker "was absolutely uncompromising. And so was my father," concurred the actor's daughter, Tara MacGowran. "And that is what they liked about each other in the way that they worked together. There was no hint of . . . 'That is good enough.' Everything had to be absolutely perfect and they were both complete perfectionists, and I guess that's why they got on so well."[43]

The director remembered MacGowran as a performer "totally dedicated to his art," unfortunately to his own detriment. The weather during the filming was so difficult to gauge "it took forever to film his scenes," said Polanski. The sequence on the causeway, in which the actor's character, Albie, has been shot in the stomach and left to wait in the car while his partner goes to get help, was especially problematic. "Jack was not only a fine actor but also a true professional and real trouper who would remain half-immersed in icy water for hours without complaint,"[44] marveled Polanski. "He of course had a wet suit under his garment because it was impossible to sit through. . . . I think it was the producer, Gene Gutowski, [who] noticed he was shivering; he was totally blue."[45]

Gutowski, whose recollections of making the film sometimes contradicted Polanski's, wholly agreed with the director about the incident. "We realized in the course of shooting he was getting bluer and bluer in the face and couldn't deliver the lines and started shivering and we carried him out," he said. "Water had gotten into the rubber suit. He would not complain, he wouldn't tell anybody—he was actually slowly freezing to death. Jack was a sparrow of a man and there was not a stitch of protective fat on him."[46]

Assistant director Roger Simons, however, questioned this account. "We went to a lot of trouble in preproduction—I remember

Jack MacGowran in his scene on the causeway. TWENTIETH CENTURY-FOX/METRO-GOLDWYN-MAYER STUDIOS

a lot of discussion going on about the safety of that—how cold it was going to be, how long he'd be in the car. I don't think Jack nearly died or was anywhere near. I would be upset if that was true because of the time we spent planning it. There's no way we'd continue at any stage if we thought Jack was not in any shape to continue." While Simons agreed about the lack of complaint from MacGowran, "I would suggest at no point was he in any danger whatsoever. In my opinion."[47]

The Irish actor's dedication to his art would win him the starring role in Polanski's next film, the eccentric Professor Abronsius in *Dance of the Vampires*. "The character of the professor was inspired by Jackie MacGowran," said the director. "I had a very hard time on *Cul-de-Sac* but I had a fantastic experience with Jack and the next script I decided to write for him." The filmmaker began making caricatures of MacGowran as the Einstein-like vampire hunter of his imagination; the performer proved a continual source of stimulation. "A lot of things in the script, a lot of ideas, were inspired by Jack's behavior and by funny things about him."[48]

Polanski would continue to be plagued by discord with actors, finding himself in conflict with John Cassavetes over every aspect of filming *Rosemary's Baby* and sending Faye Dunaway into a fit of hysterics by plucking an uncooperative hair from her head on the set of *Chinatown*—to name just two—but the abundance of problems engendered by *Cul-de-Sac* drove him to the breaking point.

Producer Gene Gutowski, Roman Polanski and writer Gérard Brach; photo by Jerry Shatzberg. RUE DES ARCHIVES 3 BIS RUE PELLEPORT PARIS/GRANGER

Polanski poses with Catherine Deneuve (left) and Françoise Dorléac at the London premiere of Repulsion. MPTVIMAGES.COM

A Japanese poster for Repulsion.

Lionel Stander and Jack MacGowran are gangsters on the lam in Cul-de-Sac. NATIONAL FILM ARCHIVE/ COMPTON FILMS

Cul-de-Sac *crew on the causeway, from left: Tommy Brooker, Roy Ford, Lionel Stander, Roman Polanski, Roger Simons, unknown, Gil Taylor, unknown.* PHOTO BY ROBIN O'DONOGHUE

Cul-de-Sac crew on castle terrace, from left: Françoise Dorléac, Roy Ford, Geoff Seaholme, Ted Sturgis (facing person in chair); right foreground: Stuart Black (?), Bridget Sellers. PHOTO BY ROBIN O'DONOGHUE

Polanski brought respectability to the presenters of Cul-de-Sac.

Love and death compete for attention on Italian poster for Cul-de-Sac. COMPTON/COLUMBIA CEIAD

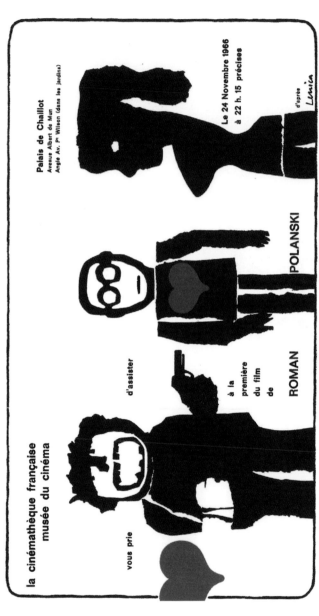

Invitation to the French premiere of Cul-de-Sac; cartoon by Jan Lenica. COURTESY OF ROMAN POLANSKI ARCHIVES

Cul-de-Sac *poster concept by artist James McNeff.*

Sharon Tate and Jack MacGowran on the set of Dance of the Vampires. PIERLUIGI PRATURLON/SHUTTERSTOCK

A DAY AT THE BEACH

Roman Polanski found himself running out of options as filming on *Cul-de-Sac* neared the end of the ninth week. The director was not only two weeks behind schedule but still had a lengthy scene to capture that would take an indeterminable amount of time. With all the back-and-forth between himself and the producer, the financiers, and the completion guarantors, there was nothing less brewing than "a catastrophe," as Polanski described it. "I wanted to do it in one shot but I wasn't telling anyone. And finally when the day came I said what I need, and I told everybody it was going to be one shot, it was going to be shot in one day instead of five or six."[1] Gil Taylor grumbled and told him it would take forever.

The extended sequence—representing 15 pages of the shooting script—would supposedly take place on the beach at dawn, with Donald Pleasence confiding to Lionel Stander the truth about his marriage, and Françoise Dorléac wandering out of camera range to go for a dip in the water. To further complicate the situation a plane was to fly overhead, with Stander mistaking it as the enigmatic Katelbach. Polanski was determined to film the scene in a single shot without a cut, plane and all, at the approach of dusk.

"Long takes are always preferable when filming emotional scenes because they enable actors to stay right inside their roles,"[2] asserted Polanski. The cast's Herculean efforts did not go unnoticed. Bill Dial of the *Atlanta Constitution*, who called the director's style "Bergmanesque," felt Pleasence and Stander's conversation on the beach was "one of the most brilliant sustained pieces of acting I've seen."[3]

Lionel Stander and Donald Pleasence converse on the beach in Cul-de-Sac.
SIGMA III/PHOTOFEST

Pages 56–71 were shot on Holy Island's north shore August 14, 1965—the last day on location. It was so cold on the beach members of the crew wore coats and gloves. The tension was thicker than the proverbial London fog and nerves were on edge. The shoot was especially difficult for Dorléac, though she had very few lines. The actress, who could not swim, was required to doff her robe and run nude into the icy North Sea and later reenter the shot.

Making the scene more problematic was the fact that Polanski insisted on recording all the original sound, noted sound camera operator Robin O'Donoghue. "So we hid microphones, we didn't have radio mics in those days—all the mics were wires, we had to build rocks that would hold microphones. So when Donald Pleasence would run to a certain area, we knew we weren't going to stop because of focus and everything. We had a rock on the beach that had a microphone in it. So when he was shouting, we'd record it.

I had the microphone, I was way down the beach. Françoise Dorléac had to run, she's naked . . . she said, 'What are you doing here?!' I said, 'I'm recording the sound.' She said, 'Don't you look. Don't look.' I said, 'I won't look.'"[4]

Dorléac had voiced no objection to baring her backside in a previous bedroom scene with Pleasence but suddenly became reluctant to go au naturel on the strand. The director assured her she would be photographed at a distance, then she expressed concern about the water being too cold. Later, when asked by a reporter about stripping for the camera, Dorléac responded, "If it has to be done for artistic reasons, because of the demands of the plot, I'll do it. For sensationalism, never."[5]

Michael Klinger reportedly showed up and suggested two takes were enough, as the director was about to begin another one. The actors were midway through the third take—by Polanski's count—and everything was just right when Gene Gutowski approached him from behind and whispered, "Françoise has fainted!" Polanski was so focused on getting what he wanted he could only think to respond,

Dorléac bares her derriere in a bedroom scene with Pleasence and Stander.
TWENTIETH CENTURY-FOX/METRO-GOLDWYN-MAYER STUDIOS

"Well, get her to unfaint!"[6] As he recalled, "My only thought was not that she might drown, but that she couldn't come back into the frame for the end of the shot."[7] When the actress didn't reappear, he was forced to cut. "It came hard because this had been the best take so far," he observed.[8] The actress reportedly began to menstruate and suffer from hypothermia as well.

Pleasence, for his part, asserted the scene "went like clockwork. We had no trouble with it. We only had three takes—the only tragedy so far as the film was concerned was that the third take was the best and we couldn't use it because poor Françoise passed out from the cold."[9]

"When they set it up, the tide was in," said O'Donoghue. "So she had to just run, not that far, to go in the sea. When they came to shoot it, the tide had gone out so it was much further for her than originally planned. So she had a much longer run. She probably got very cold."[10]

Roger Simons disagreed on the number of takes—"I think it's ten, four of them we got the plane right, six we got them wrong"—but vividly recalled the scene. "What I do remember is . . . she goes out to the water, we pan her in to the sea, we then come back to the two of them arguing on the beach and the plane goes over. In the meantime Bridget Sellers, the wardrobe mistress, runs out to the water and puts a dressing gown around her and keeps her warm, then I have to cue her back to go into the water again after about eight minutes so when we pan 'round again she comes out.

"My recollection is, I gave the cue for her to be sent back out into the water, she went back out on take ten, and when we pan 'round, she didn't appear. She was still in the water," said Simons. "We cut the shot, Roman started going, 'Where is she, where is she, why isn't she coming out of the water?' And then Bridget ran in . . . and lifted her out of the water, and everybody went running over to see her. Roman immediately knew, he was furious because he knew she'd done enough takes for her and thought we should've printed the shot, and that was her way of protesting. So she pretended to collapse—that's my opinion—and that was the end of that shot."[11]

Stander was infuriated as well, said Gutowski. "She could have died there. They were just furious with her because she ruined what they considered was a perfect take,"[12] the producer contended. "Fortunately there was a doctor among the onlookers on the beach. They took her out and pumped her heart a few times and it started and she was fine."

But all was anything but fine. "The set exploded into pandemonium," according to Barbara Leaming. "The usually aloof British crew had reached its limit."[13] The director acknowledged dissent in his memoirs, noting Pleasence went so far as to lodge a formal protest on behalf of the company. "Already quick to complain whenever they got a chance, the whole crew seized upon this incident as if it were the last straw. Françoise apparently fainted because of the cold, and they did their best to make me feel like a monster."[14]

"No," Simons countered. "He made himself look like a monster, because he was a monster to work with. But I think the crew also like myself had tremendous respect for the fact that he's a great director. . . . One has to realize we'd spent [nine] weeks there by this time. You have a developing relationship of pretty much hatred between Françoise and Roman as the film goes on. She'd been in quite difficult scenes, with Roman having a go at her. It was pretty frosty between Roman and the actors. I think they all basically loved him as I did, but it's a Roman film, he's very much in control of it. And after a while—Donald is a wonderful actor [but] you know, 50 takes and they'd had enough."[15]

Simons' assessment of the situation, and Polanski's assertion that "Françoise herself was right as rain the next day and bore me no grudge,"[16] square with Dorléac's statement to interviewer Edwin Miller: "I had to run in ice-cold water many times, and I kept doing one scene over and over again until I fainted. My pulse had practically stopped from the exposure, and a doctor who was passing by gave me an injection. But it was only my body that did not respond to the director's instructions. My spirit was willing," the actress stressed. "I would have gone on and on until he told me to stop. I could never complain. Polanski is completely preoccupied with film; he doesn't think about the actors as human beings at all. But I do not mind it; he is a brilliant director,"[17] she remarked, in a surprisingly diplomatic observation.

Logistically, Polanski's biggest challenge was not in dealing with the actors but manipulating the timing of the plane during the shot. The director was in dismay when "even Gil Taylor deserted me, insisting it couldn't be done. He invoked RAF know-how and said that getting airplanes to appear on cue was difficult to the point of impossibility."[18]

The cinematographer concurred: "getting a Tiger Moth to fly through that over the top of these people, when you've got the director and producer sniffing down your neck, you've got to get this, we can't come tomorrow," said Taylor. "My reaction is, unless you've got a helicopter, which you can time down to the second, the chances of getting a Tiger Moth to do it are very remote."[19]

"It took a day to set up," said O'Donoghue. "Roman had a soundproof booth built on the set where the camera was, so he could talk to a guy on a microphone, talking to the plane. Because the plane had to take off from the mainland, and it had to circle, but it's a distance so the soundtrack would not pick up the sound of the plane. And they timed it. So on a certain cue from Roman on a certain line of dialogue, where they're on the beach and they're shouting and they're rowing, they'd tell the guy in the booth by a signal; the guy in the booth would radio the plane and say go, he would approach. All in one shot. There's no cut to the plane."[20]

Roger Simons recalled the setup as being a bit more complex. "Because of the length of the take and the danger of us running out of film, the only way we could make it work was that the pilot would have to give the camera turnover and action cue from a pre-determined marker put in the ground. He communicated this to me via radio," said the assistant director. "Because the flyover was if memory serves over four minutes into the scene this required a lot of rehearsal and a lot of patience. The only way we could be sure we would get the scene in. We couldn't run the camera and then say 'action' to the plane, because he'd have to circle round, find a spot, and then fly in. . . . I think we rehearsed it one day and shot it the next day; I might be wrong, it might've been on one day."

Stander and Pleasence filmed the lengthy beach scene in Cul-de-Sac *in one long take.* CONSTANTIN FILM

"I think there's 10 minutes, 20 seconds in a magazine of film, that's the maximum amount of film—1,000 feet of 35mm film was the amount you had in the camera," said Simons. "So we had to work out a way with the take that long, how not to run out of film. I was standing in the sand with earphones on, I was the one who had to say 'action' to the actors; Roman always gives the 'action' but on this occasion the pilot was giving the 'action' when he hit a certain spot . . . that was the key to how the scene started."[21]

Polanski achieved what he wanted in the end. "I rehearsed the whole day and got it all right and the twilight came and we shot the scene and got it in one shot . . . and the plane came exactly on the cue when it was needed," said the director, who "would do the Cossack dance around the set," recalled Trevor Delaney, "when he was happy with a take."[22]

Critic David Sterritt has observed, "Stylistically speaking, few scenes of the sixties surpass the seven-minute sequence shot with a plane appearing in the sky at precisely the right moment; this is amazingly 'advanced cinema,' as Polanski once boasted. . . . There's no questioning the artistry of the hyperactive, ultrainventive film, which spits out more visual ideas per scene than [almost] any sixties picture."[23]

"The effort that took, to bring something new," marveled O'Donoghue. "Roman went to a lot of trouble to get good shots, interesting shots. It engendered a lot of enthusiasm. So much so the film was scheduled for [six] weeks and it went to nine weeks. Michael Klinger came up to rattle the sabers. . . . They certainly wanted to see what was going on."[24]

Gene Gutowski would remember the 7-minute-and-45-second scene as "one of those film history takes."[25] It was in fact one of the longest shots attempted up to that time, though certainly not without precedent. Alfred Hitchcock had made protracted takes not once but twice with distinction. After wowing audiences with a traveling crane shot in the climactic scene of *Young and Innocent* (1937), he achieved notoriety with *Rope* (1948), editing together a series of 10-minute shots to make the film look like one continuous take. Hitchcock however told François Truffaut in hindsight his "crazy idea to do it in a single shot . . . was quite nonsensical."[26]

While such recent films as Alejandro G. Iñárritu's *Birdman* (2014) contemporize the all-in-one concept of *Rope*, many filmmakers in the past have made their mark with the extended take. Chief among them have been Orson Welles' *Touch of Evil* (1958), which begins with a showy crane shot, Jean-Luc Godard's *Weekend* (1967), Michelangelo Antonioni's *The Passenger* (1975), Andrei Tarkovsky's *The Sacrifice* (1986), Robert Altman's *The Player* (1992), with its initial tracking shot itself poking fun at tracking shots, and Aleksandr Sokurov's *Russian Ark* (2002). The extraordinary beach shot in Polanski's *Cul-de-Sac* still stands high among them, amid the many memorable achievements of the director's seven-decade career—albeit causing great concern for some of those involved.

RELEASE AND CRITICAL RECEPTION

The year 1966 was a great one for film. Michelangelo Antonioni made *Blow-up*, arguably his best picture. Andrei Tarkovsky created his masterpiece, *Andrei Rublev*. Ingmar Bergman crafted *Persona*. Jiri Menzel turned heads with *Closely Watched Trains*. Karel Reisz created the wonderfully offbeat *Morgan!* Volker Schlöndorff made his first feature, *Young Törless*, heralding the German New Wave. John Ford made his last film, *7 Women*, which "feels less like a swansong and more like the work of a director given a new lease of life,"[1] in the words of critic Craig Williams. Jean-Luc Godard titillated us with *Masculin Féminin*. Robert Bresson enlightened us with *Au hasard Balthazar*, which Godard felt managed to "contain the world in an hour and a half."[2] And Roman Polanski gave us *Cul-de-Sac*.

A motion picture described by its director as "a great cinematic success" is rarely followed up with the admission the film was "a complete flop."[3] But *Cul-de-Sac* was unsuccessful at the box office in its original release "because people are used to specific genres and the different conventions that define them, and if you break those rules audiences aren't happy,"[4] Polanski told an interviewer.

Tony Tenser made up his mind before audiences and critics had their say. "Polanski sold [Michael] Klinger on *Cul-de-Sac* and I went along with it because I thought it was okay," he told his biographer. "The film itself wasn't much of a story but we thought we could rely on the director to put a little pep into it. By the time we saw the finished copy I knew that we had made a mistake."[5] Tenser presumably kept his opinions to himself during Compton's press conference at the Cannes Film Festival, where the film was shown unofficially just prior to its release.

In mid-October 1965, Polanski arrived in Hollywood to talk to potential distributors. The trip coincided with a visit to New York to promote *Repulsion*, before he returned to London to begin editing *Cul-de-Sac* in earnest. Among those he talked to in the film capital were representatives from Columbia Pictures, according to a report in *Variety*.

Producer Ben Kadish, an acquaintance of Gene Gutowski's who had met with Polanski in Los Angeles, would ultimately lead the film-maker to a US distribution deal for his Holy Island thriller. Having traveled to the end of the line with Compton, Polanski was looking to finance his next picture when Kadish introduced him to Martin Ransohoff and John Calley of Filmways, Inc. Ransohoff had expressed interest in Polanski the year before when they considered *Repulsion* for US distribution. "Martin was very keen to meet Polanski. I'm sure he was thinking of working with him even then,"[6] said Tenser.

Polanski began filming *Dance of the Vampires* for Ransohoff in the Italian alps late in February 1966 after being forced to switch locations from an authentic castle outside a village in Bolzano to a plateau in the Dolomites, at the last minute when a mysterious warm spell melted all the snow. As a result, the budget soared from $600,000 to more than $2 million; much of it had to be shot in man-made snow at MGM Borehamwood (where they had to build their own castle) and nearby Elstree Studios outside London. The film had been in production nearly a month when the *New York Times* and other publications reported in March Filmways' acquisition of American and Canadian rights to *Cul-de-Sac*, and their plan to release it through their distribution arm, Sigma III Corporation. The latter would take eight months to reach New York and nearly two years to arrive in Los Angeles.

Following the trade screening at Cannes, *Cul-de-Sac* had its world premiere June 2, 1966, at the Cameo-Polytechnic Cinema on Regent

Street in London's West End. Polanski attended with Sharon Tate—his costar in *Vampires*—amid a celebrity-studded crowd. The Cameo-Poly was in the same building where the Lumière Brothers had first projected moving pictures in the UK in 1896, but the venue was less

Page 8—The Daily Cinema

Tuesday 24 May 1966

CUL-DE-SAC

Roman Polanski and Lionel Stander, director and star of Compton's new British film CUL-DE-SAC, went to a recent preview of the film, to meet guests from magazines, TV and radio.

Also present were Michael Klinger and Tony Tenser, Compton chiefs.

CUL-DE-SAC is to have its premiere on 2 June at the Cameo-Poly, Regent Street.

Produced by Gene Gutowksi, it stars Donald Pleasence, Francoise Dorleac and Lionel Stander and was made entirely on location on desolate Holy Island. It is a black comedy on the triangle theme.

1. *Michael Klinger and Lionel Stander.*

2. *Tony Tenser, Lionel Stander and Peter Baker (Films and Filming).*

3. *Mr. and Mrs. Klinger with Roman Polanski.*

4. *Lionel Stander, Tony Tenser and Bill Pay (Motion Picture Herald).*

5. *Roman Polanski and Maude Spector, casting director on "Cul-de-Sac."*

6. *Roman Polanski, Lionel Stander and Freda Bruce Lockhart (Woman).*

7. *Eric Dallman with Tom Hutchinson (Nova) and Leslie Halliwell (Granada TV's 'Cinema').*

8. *Mr. and Mrs. Lionel Stander.*

ROMAN POLANSKI AT PREVIEW

Attendees at a London press preview included Michael Klinger and Lionel Stander (1), Tony Tenser (2), Roman Polanski (3), casting director Maude Spector (5), and film critic Leslie Halliwell (7, right). COURTESY OF SCREEN INTERNATIONAL prestigious than its history might indicate. The *Times* couldn't help but note in its review the exhibitors were "not long ago our most successful purveyors of cheap but effective sensationalism."[7]

As if to prove the point, Compton-Cameo had recently advertised the forthcoming premiere alongside another film of theirs, *Secrets of a Windmill Girl*, featuring a provocative image of a half-clad starlet. The British Board of Film Censors classified *Cul-de-Sac* "X," approving it for patrons older than age 16—not to be confused with the "X" rating devised by the Motion Picture Association of America two years later to designate a film displaying excessive violence or explicit sexuality such as Polanski's *What?* (*Che?*, 1973), which the *New York Times* described as "totally without redeeming social value."[8]

Compton's pressbook crudely summarized the plot of *Cul-de-Sac* for the benefit of British exhibitors and reviewers without a hint of the film's wit and inventiveness. It was often vague; Teresa's rendezvous with Christopher were referred to as "heavy flirtations." The press release noted but one comic element—Richard (Lionel Stander) being forced to pose as a butler—which reviewers would single out as well. A further release quoted Polanski and Brach's three-word summary of the film, "*L'humeur, l'amour, la mort*," dryly adding, "It does not translate well into English!"[9]

The British press, several respected film reviewers among them, were overwhelmingly negative in their response to the picture. Richard Roud, of the *Guardian*, tried to mitigate his criticism with a nod toward opposing viewpoints: "Two friends, for whose opinions I have every respect, found it an extremely entertaining work of black humour. Two more (and I) found it a really crashing bore. For some, Roman Polanski's direction was masterful; for others, adequate; for me, inept."[10] Given Roud's position as the first director of the New York Film Festival—where the filmmaker had been welcomed with open arms with *Knife in the Water*—the review must have felt particularly stinging.

Dilys Powell, considered one of the era's top critics, was equally damning in the *Sunday Times*: "Black comedy, somebody has called it; sick comedy I should have said, and not so much of the comedy either; the perversity here is not, as it is in *Modesty Blaise*, an impudent parody, it is coldly savoured, just as the cruelty in the humiliation of the husband is savoured," asserted Powell. "The situations are scarcely played for fun, black or any other kind; *Cul-de-Sac* develops rather into an essay in the psychopathic. Splendidly staged against empty sky and encircling water . . . it holds you in a claustrophobic nightmare, too well done to let you get away,"[11] she allowed.

The British critics sounded the first note on what would become a recurring theme throughout the film's release, unfavorably comparing *Cul-de-Sac* with the director's earlier work, especially his first feature. "His *Knife in the Water* seemed something bold and brilliant and most of us squawked with excitement and anticipation," wrote Isabel Quigley in the *Spectator*. However, she felt his latest film "isn't just worthless, it's pretentiously worthless, which is worse; in fact it actually seems like self-parody, with all the self-congratulatory tricks of a man going round in circles."[12]

The reviewer for the British Film Institute's *Monthly Film Bulletin* (identified only as D. W.) agreed, finding "nothing to suggest that Polanski really knew what he was aiming at. . . . And this is all the more disappointing when one notices in the film echoes of the sustained brilliance of his *Knife in the Water*."[13]

Cul-de-Sac did have its champions. Alexander Walker, writing in the *Evening Standard*, found the picture "most skillfully directed and eminently well photographed . . . the film is a rich gamut of nauseatingly tactile and abnormal sensations," he stated. "Beyond one very tedious, overlong passage near the start, it is nevertheless a hypnotic experience watching it—principally because of its own director's involvement with it."[14]

Unlike Cannes, where Polanski would wait decades for appro-
bation on a grand scale, the Berlin International Film Festival was
the scene of triumph for the second year in a row. *Cul-de-Sac* won
the Golden Bear at the 16th annual Berlinale in July. In bestowing
the top award on Britain's official entry, the international jury pre-
sided over by Pierre Bromberger acknowledged the film's artistic
energy and vividness; they affirmed as well as "the growing mastery
of Roman Polanski's directorial style."[15]

The unusually wet weather prompted comedian Milton Berle—
Hollywood's official delegate to the festival—to remark, "Berlin is
a nice place to live if you're an umbrella."[16] Though it didn't rain on
Polanski's parade, the decision to award his film first prize was not
a unanimous one. "There was some hostility to the news," observed
Variety, "but in this case the cheers were far louder than the noises
of dissent."[17] Film critic Hollis Alpert, who sat on the jury, reported,
"Discussions that were loud, long and contentious . . . the film did
not win the approval of all the members of the jury. But it won the
approval of the majority, and for reasons of its directorial skill, not to
say brilliance." The director, he insisted in defense of the prize, was
"a superb cinematic storyteller."[18]

The jury voted 8 to 1 in favor of presenting the Silver Bear best
actor award to Lionel Stander for his performance in *Cul-de-Sac*.
Unfortunately, the festival rules prohibited two major awards being
given to the same film. The actor, who was in attendance, had to
content himself with a standing ovation; Jean-Pierre Leaud, who
took home the prize for Jean-Luc Godard's *Masculin Féminin*, "was
therefore something of a compromise, and was received with little
enthusiasm," *Variety* reported.[19]

With Polanski absent (still in production on *Dance of the Vampires*), the Golden Bear ended up in financier Michael Klinger's
hands. Four decades later, Tony Tenser called his late partner's son,
Tony Klinger, to ask if he could have the trophy as well as the Silver

Bear won by *Repulsion*, or copies of the prizes. "I asked him why
he'd want them when he had been prepared to join a lawsuit against
my father to stop him making them," recalled Klinger. "He couldn't
come up with an answer."[20]

Klinger and Tenser and executive producer Sam Waynberg were
not the only ones backing the Polanski film. Another was independent German producer Erich Mehl. The influential financier, known
as the Grey Eminence in the trade, was "very much behind *Cul-de-
Sac*," *Weekly Variety* stated in a news item on the film's European
distribution. He acquired rights for Switzerland, Austria, Belgium,
Luxemburg, and the Netherlands, and had "a percentage deal with
pic's world rights. . . . His strong financial contribution also made
Repulsion possible."[21] According to the trade paper Mehl bought
rights for Germany as well, though that was reportedly Waynberg's
territory.

Cul-de-Sac was seen throughout Europe. In Germany it became
Wenn Katelbach Kommt, a precise translation of the French work-
ing title *Si Katelbach Arrive . . .* ; in Spain *Callejón sin Salida*, not to
be confused with the title given the Humphrey Bogart movie *Dead
Reckoning*. In Sweden it was called *Djävulsk gissan*, in Denmark
Blind Vej, and in Finland, *Umpikuja*. In Poland it was known as *Mat-
nia*, in Yugoslavia, *Corsokak*, in Hungary *Zsákutca*, and in the Czech
Republic *Ve Slepé Ulicce*. In Italy, where the film won the Critics
Prize at the Venice International Film Festival, death predominated
on posters—in images of Donald Pleasence shooting Lionel Stander,
and Jack MacGowran's corpse awaiting burial. The specter of darkness was in the key advertising slogan as well: "*un Delitto in Fondo
alla Strada*"[22] (A murder down the road).

The Paris premiere was held November 24, 1966, at the
Cinémathèque française, in the 16th arrondissement. Most of the
reviews were less than favorable. "To say that *Cul-de-sac* is a com-
forting film would be to lie, to say that it is a film without concessions

would be to lie more," stated *Arts* critic Pierre Marcabru, speaking for many of his colleagues. More pointedly he noted, the movie was "not always of the best taste."[23]

Pierre Billard of *L'Express* derided the filmmaker as well. "One finds, in *Cul-de-sac*, the ferocious misogyny of Polanski and his macabre humor which unleashes explosions of cutting laughter," he observed. "And the worst torture is the humiliation which Polanski repeatedly plunges his characters into with a cheerful delight."[24]

Jean Collet similarly took Polanski to task in *Télérama*: "Today I see the film of a malicious person who knows how to exploit the complexes of others. Show that life is absurd, vain, empty, ugly. Choose the very puritan England to spread your excrement on film."[25]

Underappreciated and savagely criticized though it may have been, the *Cul-de-Sac* shown in Europe was the film Polanski envisioned. The *Cul-de-Sac* audiences saw in the picture's first incarnation on US soil, just prior to the Paris opening, was not. The film was not subjected to the almost puritanical standards the British Board of Film Censors (BBFC), Hollywood's Production Code Authority, or Metro-Goldwyn-Mayer would try to impose on *Dance of the Vampires*—with the BBFC voicing concerns about "vampirism mixed up with sex, which brings in an element of sexual perversion"[26]—but its predecessor met with unexpected tampering.

Marty Ransohoff trimmed *Cul-de-Sac* for the United States though he had no legal right to touch it. "Inside almost every producer lurks a frustrated film editor, but Ransohoff, as I found to my dismay, was more than a would-be editor; he was a compulsive butcher of other people's work,"[27] Polanski recalled in his memoirs. "The premiere was already set, and it was so dramatic that I had to ship a few reels from London, which I replaced, but others remained cut. He cut very nice moody sequences which were quite important for the film."[28] As the director elaborated to one interviewer, "Atmosphere and mood were taken out, because Ransohoff felt there was no value to scenes without dialogue."[29]

The Paris premiere of Cul-de-Sac, *left to right: Françoise Dorléac, Roman Polanski, producer Gene Gutowski and writer Gérard Brach.* RUE DES ARCHIVES 3 BIS RUE PELLEPORT PARIS/GRANGER

Cul-de-Sac was 111 minutes in length (10,051 feet) when it opened in London, as indicated by the BFI *Monthly Film Bulletin*. In New York it ran 104 minutes according to the *New York Daily News*, though Ransohoff cut it as much as 10 minutes by Polanski's calculations. The *Daily News* telegraphed its verdict in the headline ("Offbeat, Sick")[30] when the picture opened November 7 at Loew's Tower East on Manhattan's Upper East Side, but it was the *New York Times* and its influential critic, Bosley Crowther, to whom filmgoers paid attention. The running time was the least of their concerns.

Crowther, who had called *Repulsion* "An absolute knockout of a movie,"[31] felt *Cul-de-Sac* failed to measure up to the director's previous features, in step with many of his European colleagues. To be fair, he found "this lunatic commotion" was not without "certain recommendations." He allowed that "Mr. Polanski has directed with impressive ingenuity and comic speed. But what does it all add up to," he asked his avid readers, "when the end of the clowning is reached and the naughtiness has been exculpated in a hideous spitting-up of blood? Is Mr. Polanski endeavoring to tell us anything about life or crime or perversion in this complex and terminally morbid joke? If he is, I sure don't get it—except maybe that people are sick, that even good humor isn't funny and that social sterility is."[32]

Joseph Gelmis asserted the film was "certain to offend those who take it literally" in *Newsday* but thought audiences should forgive the director his "sophomoric excesses," given the picture's "perverse originality and devious brilliance."[33] Andrew Sarris of the *Village Voice* felt Polanski was determined "to outrage his audience at all costs."[34] Brendan Gill called the film "the quintessence of fashionable, phony moviemaking" in the *New Yorker*, and blasted away at it: "A slick, gaudily Gothic movie, it seems bent on making our flesh creep . . . the contempt [Polanski and Brach] feel for us is remarkably frank. Nothing is so preposterous that they do not count on us to swallow it. Gross absurdity is piled on gross absurdity—our fault if we choke."[35]

However, it was Crowther whose slings and arrows cut the deepest. The preeminent critic of his era would resign his three-decade post the following year, not long after attacking *Bonnie and Clyde* for a blend of comedy and violence "as pointless as it is lacking in taste"[36]—but not quite soon enough. Not content with his first pan of *Cul-de-Sac*, he took a second punch at it in an extended essay two weeks later. Although he allowed there was "some wickedly droll dialogue," he dismissed it as "a grotesque conglomeration of crime melodrama, slapstick farce, surrealistic social comment and psychoneurotic exposé."[37]

He speculated Polanski had been given a big budget with "no strings attached to that lovely pile of British pounds," but reckoned, "there isn't a smidgen of logic or purpose in the whole morbid thing, outside of the purpose of shocking and dumbfounding the customers." The newspaper advertisements tweaked Crowther's words into an endorsement. "After two clean hits . . . Polanski is entitled to one wild swing"[38] became "Polanski's wild swing!" bolstered by his comment about the filmmaker's "impressive ingenuity."

Judith Crist, reputedly "the critic most-hated by Hollywood,"[39] was equally severe in the *New York World Journal Tribune*: "You get the fleeting notion that maybe this young Polish director is kidding. But no. He's dead earnest all the way, apparently convinced that perversion, mayhem, necrophilia, nymphomania, homosexuality, sadism, murder and a variety of mental disorders are the stuff 'bizarre comedy' is made on." Crist called the film a big disappointment and

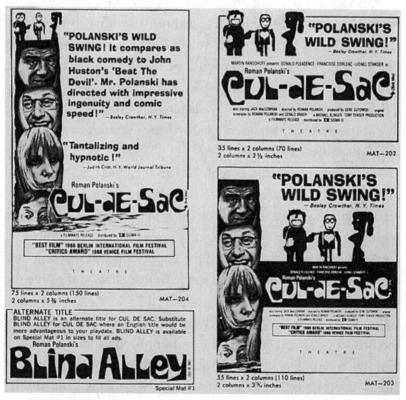

Ads from the US pressbook for Cul-de-Sac. SIGMA III/USC CINEMA-TELEVISION LIBRARY

groused it was a waste of the director's talent, that it would prove entertaining only "for those who can laugh while fighting off nausea." She concluded, "No. Mr. Polanski isn't kidding. Perhaps the jurors at Berlin were."[40] Yet she was also quoted favorably in ads: "Tantalizing and hypnotic!"

Another piece of upbeat advertising copy, created by Sigma III's marketing department, read, "Sometimes there's nothing left to do but laugh!" The distributor encouraged exhibitors to substitute the film's alternate title, *Blind Alley*, "where an English title would be more advantageous."[41] Apparently it was little used, except for such occasions as the headline on the *Chicago Tribune* review: "'Blind Alley' Is a Dead End."[42]

Polanski did not take the reviews lightly. Asked to reflect on the film's failure to attract audiences three years after its release, he observed, "They are not up to it yet. This film, if it were shown this year or two years from now, would be much better received. The critics in New York, especially, were too square for *Cul-de-Sac*. They didn't understand it, I think." He lambasted Crowther for "a piece that was extremely dishonest" and writing "whatever came to his mind" regardless of the facts.

He lashed out at Crist as well. "If you read her original reviews of my first two [feature] films, she didn't like those either, so why was she so disappointed in *Cul-de-Sac*?" As he told an interviewer regarding her laundry list of negative terms, "I don't remember all the 'isms she saw in it, but I had the impression that maybe a new dictionary had just been printed in the United States at the time she wrote her review."[43]

Though *Cul-de-Sac* survived the cold shoulder it received from the British press and continued to run for months in London, the film was "almost literally blasted out of the theatre" in New York—as Hollis Alpert noted in the *Saturday Review*—thanks to "unnecessarily harsh reviews"[44] from name-brand critics. *Variety*'s report on the

Tower East's first week's box office receipts was a polite understatement: "First session finished Sunday was nice $9,400, if not up to hopes."[45]

Jiří Menzel's *Closely Watched Trains*, the 1966 Czech film that went on to win the Academy Award for Best Foreign Film in 1968, had more in common with *Cul-de-Sac* than its off-kilter blend of comic and dramatic elements and the Eastern bloc background of its director. Both were released in the United States by producer-distributor Leonard S. Gruenberg, who headed Sigma III, but their paths diverged markedly.

The film prizes earned in Berlin and Venice did little to enhance *Cul-de-Sac*'s reputation in the Western Hemisphere. Nor did the awards attract the attention of the Academy of Motion Picture Arts and Sciences, though the director had been on their radar since *Knife in the Water*. The film was not without recognition in the English-speaking world, however; BAFTA nominated Gilbert Taylor for Best Cinematography-Black & White.

The film was seen in Washington, DC, in February 1967 but did not arrive in Chicago until Christmas week—a not unusual delay for European films, according to Roger Ebert, who noted in the *Chicago Sun-Times* the Windy City was apparently "trapped in a time warp" in that regard. Ebert felt the film had "an eerie appeal"[46] but neglected to mention the most haunting element—Françoise Dorléac was already in her grave, the victim of a tragic auto accident that had taken her life that summer at the age of 25.

Unsurprisingly, *Cul-de-Sac* did not appear in *Variety*'s report of highest-grossing films (or biggest rentals, as the top box office successes were then designated) for 1966 or 1967. Michelangelo Antonioni's *Blow-Up*, a quirky art house movie that invites comparison to the Polanski film, was released in January 1967 and became a critics' darling; it also went on to become the top foreign release of the year, reporting rentals of $5.9 million.

That the film did not reach Melbourne, Australia, until the summer of 1968 is not surprising; its failure to materialize in Los Angeles until January of that year is downright baffling. Though its forthcoming run had been advertised in December, it failed to play the all-important Oscar-qualifying engagement. By the time the awards race rolled around for films released in 1968, *Cul-de-Sac* had been forgotten by voters—unlike *Blow-Up*, which was nominated for screenplay and direction. It was also competing against another Polanski film with a major studio behind it—*Rosemary's Baby*.

Kevin Thomas of the *Los Angeles Times* gave the earlier film one of its more even-handed reviews when it finally opened at the Los Feliz Theatre in the Hollywood area, on a double bill with Tad Danielewski's 1962 adaptation of Jean-Paul Sartre's *No Exit*. "What gives *Cul-de-Sac* its sharp definition is its realism. Polanski . . . never indulges in unneeded symbolism or any other gratuitous devices. As a result, he leaves us with the feeling that because his people are three-dimensional we can see in them all the sadness and folly of mankind."[47]

Martin Ransohoff's unauthorized re-edit of *Cul-de-Sac* would pale in comparison to the hatchet job performed on *Dance of the Vampires* in North America, where the film would be haphazardly released in a mutilated version as *The Fearless Vampire Killers or Pardon Me, But Your Teeth Are in My Neck*. Longtime MGM Supervising Editor Margaret Booth and MGM Head of Theatrical Post Production Merle Chamberlain were the alleged culprits in recutting the film and redubbing the actors' voices,[48] according to the studio's one-time head negative cutter, Michael J. Sheridan. (However, Sheridan "may have his own axe to grind against the MGM post production department of the time," noted writer Glenn Erickson.[49] Ransohoff, who was based in England at the time, was blamed for years.)

Much the same fate suffered by *Cul-de-Sac* in its US release would befall *Vampire Killers*, which finally surfaced in Los Angeles at midnight screenings in September 1968, 10 months after its US premiere in New York. Charles Champlin of the *Los Angeles Times* found it praiseworthy even in its mangled version, secreted into town like a corpse in the dead of night. Adding insult to injury, it would be exhumed the following year to be paired with *Valley of the Dolls* for a double bill exploiting the tragic murder of Sharon Tate.

ACTORS AND ASSESSMENTS

The director of *Cul-de-Sac* has always prized actors and considered their talents all-important to realizing his vision. As the *Daily Telegraph* observed in its review of the film, "A superbly executed and conceived character study this, owing more to the actors than the authors."[50] Critics were of disparate minds about the contributions of the cast, however.

While *Variety* noted, "Performances give a great fillip to this always absorbing, offbeat comedy drama,"[51] Nina Hibbin stated in the *Morning Star*, "The direction . . . is so clumsy and insensitive that even outstanding actors like Lionel Stander and Donald Pleasence are laid low."[52] The *Los Angeles Times*' Kevin Thomas could not have disagreed more. "As much as by the disquieting imagination of Polanski and Brach, *Cul-de-Sac* is sustained by the extraordinary performances of Pleasence and Stander," he wrote. "Pleasence's stuttering terror and Stander's boisterous, blundering menace elicit a sense of pathos and humor that puts most other so-called black comedies well into the shade."[53]

The lead actor himself polarized the critics. "It is Donald Pleasence, bald as an egg, his eyes darting behind steel-rimmed glasses like trapped ferrets, who leaves the deepest impression," noted Cecil Wilson of the *Daily Mail*.[54] Les Wedman praised his "magnificent" portrayal of "one of the most miserable, pathetic and forlorn characters ever invented. He is an astonishing actor," the critic observed in the *Vancouver Sun*.[55] "Particularly irritating is the central per-formance of Donald Pleasence," asserted D. W. in the *Monthly Film Bulletin*. "It could be seen as a brilliant piece of characterisation . . . unfortunately it leaves only the impression of a sustained piece of self-indulgence."[56]

While Roger Ebert found the actor "hilarious and frightening as a man going mad"[57] and Bosley Crowther thought he was "grotesquely amusing,"[58] at least one member of Pleasence's family found it hard to stomach. As his longtime agent, Joy Jameson, recalled, "I'm not sure how Donald felt about playing the lead in Polanski's *Cul-de-Sac* but his then wife Josephine threw up outside the cinema after seeing it."[59]

By contrast with Pleasence's mixed reviews, his costar drew over-whelmingly favorable notices. "It is Lionel Stander who is nothing short of amazing. The character is, more or less, a compilation of all the classic heavies of the last fifty years," raved Dane Lanken of the *Montreal Gazette*. Despite uttering "an unending series of tough cli-chés . . . he exhibits all the necessary respect and even tenderness for the guys who are on his side. The part should become the ultimate example for anyone who plays the bad guy in any movie to come."[60]

The *Sunday Telegraph*'s Robert Robinson was reminded of a TV cartoon character, noting, "Lionel Stander plays the gangster like Yogi-Bear enduring a plague of bees."[61] Les Wedman felt it was "by far the most revealing study he's ever done on the screen."[62] To Roger Ebert, he resembled a true movie icon: "Stander looks amazingly like Frankenstein."[63]

Time's anonymous reviewer had similar thoughts: "Stander, in the funniest and most sinister performance of his long career, plays the gangster as an amiable, fair-minded monster. . . . At 58, this mag-nificent crum-bum comic looks like King Kong after 30 years of marriage to Fay Wray, and when he opens his mouth he sounds like that genial gorilla gargling street-cars."[64]

The female lead drew by far the harshest reviews of the triumvirate. Clifford Terry (*Chicago Tribune*) claimed Françoise Dorléac "spends most of her time . . . rendering her dialogue unintelligibly."[65] The *New Yorker*'s Brendan Gill, who blasted the film as "an odious freak show," said in conclusion, "Pleasence and Stander overact outrageously, and Miss Dorléac provides a certain balance by not troubling to act at all."[66] Ann Pacey, of the gossipy British newspaper the *Sun*, was one of the few critics who had anything kind to say: "Miss Dorléac has an arresting face and a suggestion of ruthlessness appropriate to the part. But they are all involved in a strange dance to a dead end."[67]

As might be expected, the French reviewers were somewhat kinder to their countrywoman. Michel Aubriant of *Paris Presse* was clearly obsessed with "le derrière de Mlle Françoise Dorléac," which he compared with Brigitte Bardot's posterior. But she had "other attractions and other charms: beautiful eyes with dark circles and the long rebellious hair of a female in the wind. She is funny and she is crazy. She is serious and she is crazy. She can play everything: the madcap, the bitch and the romantic. This is our Shirley MacLaine."[68]

Stander's sidekick won a handful of positive notices. *Variety*'s Rich observed, "Jack MacGowran, who plays the stooge gangster, has only short exposure, but plays the role with style."[69] Patrick Gibbs of the *Daily Telegraph* observed that Albie "is given a kind of comic pathos by that excellent and bird-like little actor, Jack MacGowran."[70] The players of smaller parts did not go entirely unnoticed by the press. Leo Sullivan of the *Washington Post*, who found the film "outrageously comical," remarked, "An excellently chosen supporting cast seems to reflect more than a little bit of what Polanski thinks of his British hosts."[71]

REVIVAL AND REASSESSMENT

Film historian Danny Peary, in his 1993 book *Alternate Oscars*, judged *Cul-de-Sac* the Best Picture of 1966. ("Award Worthy Runners-Up: None.") Like both *A Man for All Seasons* and *Who's Afraid of Virginia Woolf?*, two Oscar-winning films that came out the same year, the author observed Polanski's film "contains scene after scene of confrontational power-play conversations; like [*Seasons*] it is, in a distorted way, about a man who loses everything while battling for his integrity . . . and like [*Woolf*] it uses the catalytic appearance of intruders/visitors into a couple's home to cause them to confront what's drastically wrong with their marriage." Ultimately, Peary maintained, *Cul-de-Sac* "isn't at all like either film or anything else released in 1966."[1]

Little seen in its initial US release due to haphazard distribution and scathing reviews, *Cul-de-Sac* began to build a reputation as a cult picture soon after *Rosemary's Baby* made its director a household name in 1968. The stylish Hollywood horror movie's success at the box office was undeniable, despite its dismissal in some quarters as the "most distasteful motion picture of the year."[2]

Tasteless or otherwise, the blockbuster focused attention on the filmmaker behind it: "Thus, an earlier Polanski film, like *Cul-de-Sac*, though unquestionably a masterpiece in itself, assumes new significance. Its twists of horror and peculiarity may now be seen as precedents," asserted critic Dane Lanken in the *Montreal Gazette*. Lanken also felt the older picture contained "some of the funniest and or most tragic interpersonal situations ever put on film."[3]

At the other end of Canada, Les Wedman described the picture as "a brilliant and bizarre mixture of black Polish humor and sharp social satire honed to the point where watching it is like sitting in on an autopsy. Only here it is a living dead man that he is dissecting." In one of the best reviews the film received before its Blu-ray release more than four decades later, the *Vancouver Sun* critic continued: "Polanski, with an amazing grasp of the English character and language since *Repulsion*, commands not only respect but complete admiration for the way in which he strips bare the inner emotions of his characters."[4]

Though *Cul-de-Sac* was not exactly the film its creator intended audiences to see, at least the version being shown in North America, the reassessment had begun. In a major *Film Comment* article on British films of the 1960s and '70s, critic Raymond Durgnat observed the director was "at his most brilliant as a parodist in *Cul-de-Sac*."[5]

Interest in the movie increased exponentially in the United States, along with *The Fearless Vampire Killers*. The films became in demand in 16mm screenings—the secondary format of choice before the advent of home video. Because the two titles were "the hardest to see Polanski films, they tended to get the most play in 16mm regional and college film society venues,"[6] noted artist and film historian Stephen R. Bissette.

Cul-de-Sac was trimmed further after its initial New York release, cut to 100 minutes according to an extant film rental catalogue page; the offering was labeled "A Martin Ransohoff Presentation," further rubbing salt in the wound. The film nonetheless became a draw, not only on college campuses but also in art house cinemas that specialized in revivals. The critical and commercial success of *Chinatown* (1974) of course did not hurt.

Venues like the Elgin Cinema in New York City (renowned for its "midnight movies") and the Nuart Theatre in Los Angeles showed *Cul-de-Sac* regularly throughout the 1970s, invariably on double bills with *Knife in the Water*, *Repulsion*, or *Vampire Killers*. The Cinema Lumiere in Toronto ran it in tandem with *Andy Warhol's Bad*; the Fox Venice in Los Angeles paired it with Fellini's *La Strada*.

When the Nuart screened the film in 1977, nearly a decade after its L.A. premiere, Kevin Thomas of the *Los Angeles Times* called it "delightfully odd" and compared it favorably to the other movie on the bill—an obscure sex comedy from the same director. "Unfortunately, *What?* is nonsensical without being the least amusing or inspired. (Ironically, *Cul-de-Sac* possesses the very quality of macabre whimsy so severely lacking in *What?*)"[7]

By the time Manhattan's Film Forum included *Cul-de-Sac* in a five-week series of films by Andrzej Wajda and other Polish directors in 1983, revival screenings of the picture were becoming less frequent. Revival cinemas themselves were disappearing thanks to home video—where the film was nowhere to be found, at least in the United States. The 1989 Polanski retrospective at the La Jolla Museum of Contemporary Art in San Diego, California, consisting of his 13 feature films to date, was among the more high-profile screenings of the decade.

The video revolution brought *Cul-de-Sac* into film enthusiasts' living rooms for the first time, at least in Europe and South America. The British video was coveted by US film enthusiasts from the moment it was first issued, in a 100-minute version by Stablecane Ltd. in 1985. The picture would not see video release in the United States for decades, nor could European PAL system VHS tapes be played in machines of US manufacture. The Brazilian version (*Armadilha do Destino*), which ran a mere 95 minutes, was released in the NTSC system compatible with American VCRs; relatively few potential US buyers took advantage of the fact, though enterprising shops like Videotheque in Los Angeles sold imported copies of the movie.

With the advance of DVD, the film found widespread release, winning new admirers in Britain, France, Germany, The Netherlands,

Italy, Poland, Russia, Australia, South Korea, and Japan. In their efforts to market the film, British, French, and Italian video companies anointed Jacqueline Bisset—who had emerged as a star a few short years after the film's release—with billing among the leading players despite her minimal screen time.

Anchor Bay Entertainment U.K. Ltd. issued the film on DVD in 2003, in an edition notable for one of its bonus features—*Two Gangsters and an Island*, a short documentary produced by Carl Daft for Blue Underground Ltd. Polanski, cinematographer Gil Taylor, producer Gene Gutowski, and others were interviewed about location scouting, casting, and other behind-the-scenes aspects of the film.

Deemed appropriate for 16-year-olds when originally released, *Cul-de-Sac* was considered suitable for viewers of 15 when it was first issued on videotape in the UK. With the 2003 DVD release, the BBFC lowered the age to 12, rating it for "moderate language, moderate violence and nudity." The "moderate language" in question comprised "two uses of 'bitch' and one of 'whores.' Milder language includes the use of 'bastard,' 'bloody,' 'shit' and 'son of a bitch.'"[8]

Apart from enterprising video hounds who availed themselves of bootleg copies or imported a PAL system, US viewers had little chance to see *Cul-de-Sac* at this point in time. Ironically, Anchor Bay was the British arm of an independent US distributor. Interest in the film had grown considerably in recent years, not least because *The Pianist* (2002) won the prestigious Palm d'Or at the Cannes Film Festival and brought Polanski the Academy Award for Best Director.

Marking something of a sea change in British reception to the movie, blogger Priscilla Eyles called *Cul-de-Sac* an "underrated gem" in 2009, further noting it was "a brilliantly funny, dark, and deliciously surreal film that will stay in the mind long after watching."[9]

Despite its obscurity, the film was not entirely forgotten in the United States. On the occasion of a rare screening in the State University of New York's Classic Film Series in 2004, Kevin Hagopian observed the picture was "a sixties happening colliding headlong with a film noir, *The Desperate Hours* on acid, the whole thing organized by Roman Polanski's youthful but already perverse consciousness. . . . *Cul-de-Sac* is Polanski at his best early form."[10]

In 2011 the Criterion Collection gave the film a long-overdue release in the US market, on both DVD and Blu-ray. Approved by Polanski, the 112-minute "definitive edition" (which included *Two Gangsters and an Island* and a 1967 BBC TV interview) consisted of a 2K digital transfer from the original 35mm fine-grain master positive, with the soundtrack remastered at 24-bit. "We work with Roman on every release," noted producer Karen Stetler. "We work with him to make sure the master looks the way he wants it to look. He always looks at our masters."[11]

The Criterion release introduced *Cul-de-Sac* to large numbers of people who had never had the opportunity to see it before. "This is such an odd little movie. I can completely understand why some didn't take to it when it was released," observed reviewer Ron Deutsch. "You can't describe *Cul-de-Sac* to someone. It's a movie you just have to watch and experience. And that's a pretty good description of Polanski's vision of 'true cinema.'"[12]

Critic Mike Wilmington called it "one of the great English-language films of the sixties and a classic of neo-noir . . . a unique and mesmerizing film that doesn't contain a single boring moment or one unexciting frame. It's a film Polanski long described it [*sic*] as his own personal favorite—and as highly as I esteem both *Chinatown* and *The Pianist*, I agree with him," he said. "Polanski's amazing camera eye (subjective and eerie) and his sense of the macabre, awful underpinnings of our lives . . . endow *Cul-de-sac* with qualities, visual and dramatic and even philosophical, that flawlessly recall the dark side of the sixties, of the British class system, and of life."[13]

Blogger Nathaniel Thompson (*Mondo Digital*) acknowledged it was not for everyone but lavished it with praise. "Blessed with one of his best casts and a sterling crew behind the camera, this may not be a film for all tastes (what Polanski film is?), but lovers of the offbeat will cherish this poisonous little treat. . . . A long overdue release in America, this one may not be the ideal place for Polanski newcomers to start, but for anyone with an adventurous streak, this is one of the key cult releases of the year."[14]

Screenwriter Kim Morgan (*Nightmare Alley*) enthused in her *Sunset Gun* blog, "The superb *Cul-de-sac* is [Polanski's] bats in the belfry, bat shit crazy house picture and what weird, sexy, subversive, screwy fun it all is. Party at this twisted abode? I'm there . . . the perversity, stark beauty, the isolation, the bleakness, the menacing sexuality and the insanity make the whole experience a black humored good time. A romp, in fact. It's oppressive and ominous, of course, but a special kind of Roman romp."[15]

Critic David Sterritt (*Cineaste*), who called Polanski "a cinematic imp of the perverse," observed, "*Cul-de-Sac* may not be a truly great film, but it's a truly great thingamajig, unique in its virtues and demerits alike, and unsparing in its critique of so-called normality and morality in the ever-more-decadent modern world."[16]

Cul-de-Sac is perhaps the quintessential cult film, by definition one whose audience has "a deep and irrational zeal," according to writer Josh Rottenberg. The once difficult if not impossible to see Polanski picture—which enjoyed a high-profile screening at the 2017 Cinémathèque française retrospective devoted to the director in Paris—is now a celebrated film in an era when "the long tail of home video that once gave oddball movies a shot at a glorious cult afterlife has shortened to the point of vanishing," as Rottenberg elegiacally put it.[17]

The film is far from universally embraced by today's audiences, however, as Polanski retrospectives at London's British Film Institute and New York City's Museum of Modern Art in recent years have made clear. "Reactions to *Cul-de-Sac* generally fall into two categories. People either think it's a hilarious black comedy, or 'WTF was *that* about?'"[18] said Lionel Stander's daughter, Bella Stander. "I'm in the first group, but . . . I went to the MoMA screening a few years ago with some friends, and an elderly friend who'd known my father. She was just gobsmacked."[19]

ECHOES AND SHADOWS

The abiding legacy of *Cul-de-Sac* may be in the large number of films that have been influenced or inspired by it in one way or another, just as many scholars and critics have found echoes of earlier films, books, and plays in the Polanski movie; from Shakespeare to the Coen brothers, the examples are staggering. The director also anticipated many of his own pictures.

When the British Film Institute screened *Cul-de-Sac* as part of a 2013 retrospective, Simon Columb likened George (Donald Pleasence) to Gollum in J. R. R. Tolkien's *The Hobbit*, "perched atop of the rock, crying out about his own fate. He has lost the love he adored—not through the actions of others—but through his own inaction," Columb observed. "You need only look to the end of *Chinatown* to see a striking parallel—as Jack Nicholson looks to his love, and sadness overwhelms him. They have lost their love—and they blame themselves. Though Nicholson's [Gittes] is not alone, George is—and as the credits roll on the top of George's misery it would be wrong to let him wallow in his own sadness. We want to comfort him a little and tell him: Forget it George, it's Lindisfarne."[20]

The scene in *Cul-de-Sac* wherein Teresa (Françoise Dorléac) dresses George in her nightgown and applies makeup to his face anticipates *The Tenant*, with the director himself cross-dressing in the title role. Based on a surrealist novel by Roland Topor, *The Tenant* also invites comparisons to *Repulsion*, with its protagonist going mentally unhinged, but as Polanski has pointed out, the film is in a "different register. *Repulsion* was not [meant to be] funny."[21]

Cul-de-Sac's lipstick scene is replicated in the director's *Venus in Fur*, in a moment of sexual humiliation between the male and female leads. The humiliation that permeates *Cul-de-Sac* returns in a more titillating fashion in *Bitter Moon*, however, with its focus on the relationship between an older man and a younger woman whose "disconcerting blend of sexual maturity and childish naïveté" is more than a little suggestive of Dorléac's Teresa. The couple's tumultuous relationship similarly goes sour in *Bitter Moon*, albeit in a far more shocking conclusion.

The resemblance between *Cul-de-Sac* and Polanski's *Death and the Maiden* extends beyond the three-character cast and the remote location. Sigourney Weaver taunts and torments Ben Kingsley exactly the way Lionel Stander does Françoise Dorléac and Donald Pleasence—to whom Kingsley bears a striking resemblance. And as always, the sexual tension is just barely under the surface.

The titular figure in Shakespeare's *Macbeth* "feels unhappy and unsafe in his castle,"[22] like *Cul-de-Sac*'s George, observed Ewa Mazierska. Paul Coates suggested Teresa may be "akin to Lady Macbeth, who also reproaches her husband for not being a man."[23] Roger Ebert was reminded of *Hamlet* by the grave-digging scene.

With its abundance of chickens and their by-products, *Cul-de-Sac* recalls playwright Eugene Ionesco's *The Future is in Eggs* (*L'Avenir est dans Les Oeufs*). The one-act play has a stage direction that sounds as though it could have been written by Polanski: "All this must produce in the audience a feeling of embarrassment, awkwardness and shame."[24]

"Knowing Polanski's penchant for classic horror imagery," Glenn Erickson commented in an essay on the Turner Classic Movies website, "we suspect that George is made to look like one of the male pinheads that passes for female in Tod Browning's *Freaks*."[25]

The Desperate Hours (1955) only superficially resembles *Cul-de-Sac* in the beginning, with Fredric March's ranch-style house situated on a sunny residential street in middle America. But as Humphrey Bogart makes a desperate long-distance phone call and expects someone to pay him a visit as a result, stashes his car in the family's garage, and orders the woman of the house to cook a chicken found in the refrigerator, the similarities become more and more apparent. Director William Wyler wanted an ambivalent feeling that would create "almost unbearable tension,"[26] adding to the suspense, and the likeness between the two films.

Ewa Mazierska has pointed out similarities between *Cul-de-Sac* and Jean-Luc Godard's 1959 film, *Breathless*: "In his classic, Godard also used a gangster-on-the-run formula to create a very personal and idiosyncratic film. . . . Moreover, Godard, not unlike Polanski, casts a foreign actress (the American Jean Seberg) as an amoral and beautiful female lead—a woman who lures men to their doom without blinking an eye."[27]

Leslie Stevens' *Private Property* (1960), a small independent US film that went almost unnoticed on its original release, anticipates Polanski's early work in a startling way. This tightly wound film noir suggests *Cul-de-Sac* in its depiction of two lowlife creeps who insinuate themselves into a housewife's picture-perfect but bored existence; as a bonus, a knife in the water literally figures in the plot. Ironically, Michael Klinger and Tony Tenser would choose the movie to open their Compton Cinema Club in London, one day using their profits to finance *Repulsion* and *Cul-de-Sac*.

Sam Peckinpah's *Straw Dogs* (1971) invites comparisons to *Cul-de-Sac* on several fronts. There are obvious parallels in the story of an American mathematician (Dustin Hoffman) living with his sexy young British wife in a village in Cornwall; Hoffman's repressed, inarticulate David is clearly akin to Pleasence's George, albeit more violent (not to mention heroic) in the film's climax. Critic Fernando F. Croce called the Peckinpah film "a belligerent anagram"[28] of *Cul-de-Sac*.

Filmmakers Joel and Ethan Coen have acknowledged a debt to Polanski. In an interview with *Positif* they were asked about the screening of *Barton Fink* (1991) at the Cannes Film Festival, where Polanski served as the head of the jury. "It is ironic that it was up to him to pass judgment on a film where *The Tenant* and *Cul-de-Sac* meet *Repulsion*," the interviewers noted. "Obviously, we have been influenced by his films," said Joel Coen. "The three films you mention are ones we've been quite taken by. *Barton Fink* does not belong to any genre, but it does belong to a series, certainly one that Roman Polanski originated."[29] The quirky black humor of the Coens' *Fargo* (1996) also recalls *Cul-de-Sac*.

More than one reviewer felt Ted Demme's black comedy *The Ref* (1994) was inspired by *Cul-de-Sac*. Critic Andy Klein described the Demme movie, in which a mismatched couple is taken hostage by a cat burglar (Denis Leary), as a "Disneyfied version"[30] of the Polanski film, despite many dissimilarities. It comes closest when the squabbling couple makes Leary pose as their marriage counselor in front of dinner guests.

David Mackenzie's *The Last Great Wilderness* (2003) is "heavily in debt to the same absurdist black comedy elements" present in *Cul-de-Sac*, asserted film critic Alexander Walker. The later film is set among the "wasteland hills" of Scotland. Polanski's gangsters are reimagined as "a lawless contemporary couple," a cuckolded ex-husband and a crude gigolo who will eventually don lipstick and a nightgown. Walker concluded *Wilderness* was poorly crafted and "far too literal to conjure up the ambiguous unease of the Polanski template."[31]

In his review of Michael Haneke's home invasion drama *Funny Games* (2007), critic Owen Gleiberman pinpointed "the house-party torture games"[32] of *Cul-de-Sac* as one of many antecedents. Haneke's same-named 1997 Austrian film and his almost shot-by-shot English-language remake made several apparent references to the Polanski film. Tim Roth's wimp of a husband is named George— coincidence or homage? Ulrich Mühe's Georg in the first version is strongly reminiscent of Donald Pleasence with his intensity and nervous uneasiness, though he's not as ineffectual as Roth is in the remake. The invader's borrowing and then dropping of eggs early on in both films seems like a sly homage. Even the black humor has a familiar tone: when Roth's wife (Naomi Watts) asks, "Why don't you just kill us?" one of the young attackers responds, "You shouldn't forget the importance of entertainment."

Martin McDonagh's *In Bruges* (2008) is a black comedy reminiscent of *Cul-de-Sac* in the influence of Beckett on its absurdist sense of humor. It's also about a disparate pair of hit men who bungle a job and are forced to wait for instructions from their boss, here in the medieval Belgian town of Bruges. At least one viewer noted "strong nods to Pinter's *The Dumb Waiter* and Polanski's *Cul-de-Sac*."[33]

The Thing (2009) is a music video based on the same-named song by the alternative pop/rock band The Pixies. The video, comprised of a mash-up of scenes from *Cul-de-Sac*, is not an official release by the band but the work of an apparent fan; it may be found on YouTube now and again.

Paul Rooney's short film *Still at Large* (2015), an essay about Holy Island commissioned by Berwick Visual Arts in Northumberland, includes "a dreamlike encounter" with the making of *Cul-de-Sac*. A mysterious female voice describes a fugitive who has returned "in order to re-create a moment from his childhood, when he witnessed a film being shot near Lindisfarne Castle in which a criminal is gunned down and a car goes up in flames."[34] The film was hacked and reedited in 2018.

THE WRAP PARTY

Three of *Cul-de-Sac*'s four stars continued careers already in high gear when their services were no longer required on the film, going on to greater regard and renown. The fourth, sadly, derailed a short time later. Several members of the crew would go on to work with Polanski on other films. One ended up working—albeit much to his dismay—on one of the most popular movies of modern times.

Donald Pleasence

Cul-de-Sac remains a high-water mark among Pleasence's films of the 1960s, though the era was studded with noteworthy portrayals. Roles included the title character in *Dr. Crippen* (1964), an unhappily married man who accidentally kills his wife; a whisky-loving visionary in John Sturges' wacky comedy *The Hallelujah Trail* (1965); the devious head doctor of a specialized medical team in *Fantastic Voyage* (1966); Ernst Blofield, the scar-faced, cat-stroking archvillain of the SPECTRE crime syndicate in *You Only Live Twice* (1967), opposite Sean Connery as James Bond; and Preacher Quint, the vengeful religious fanatic bent on killing Charlton Heston in Tom Gries' *Will Penny* (1968).

Blofield and Quint paid lip service to Pleasence's emergence as a movie bad guy during the decade. "I have never been particularly flattered by the roles I have been asked to play in films," he told a reporter, referring to a TV movie wherein "my character was described as a contemptuous over-fed toad. I don't think of myself in such unsavory terms but that's the type of role I usually end up playing. I suppose it's the way I look."[1] As he observed to another writer: "I don't view the human race through rose-coloured spectacles, so I find the villain more interesting to play and more three-dimensional."[2]

The year 1967 brought the actor back to the London stage in *The Man in the Glass Booth*, adapted by his friend Robert Shaw from his novel. The play, with Pleasence's Adolf Eichmann-like Nazi war criminal—and his alter ego, a Jewish tycoon—at its center, "held its first-night audience at the St. Martin's in rapt attention," observed Thomas Quinn Curtiss in the *New York Times*. "As its many-faced protagonist, Mr. Pleasence created a character of enormous resourcefulness and frenzied vitality."[3]

The play brought him his third Tony nomination a year later when the play transferred to New York (the second was for his turn as a psychotic public prosecutor in Jean Anouilh's *Poor Bitos*). In shameful Hollywood fashion he was passed over for "somebody more romantic"[4] (Maximilian Schell) when the play was made into a film, though Shaw had written it for him.

The 1970s brought a change of pace, with Pleasence debuting in a new role—the author of a children's book, *Scouse the Mouse*—and landing a greater variety of film parts as well: the sympathetic boss of the titular factory worker in George Lucas' futuristic 1971 science fiction film *THX 1138*; the narrow-minded father of innocent-but-pregnant teen Carol Kane in World War II Canada, in *Wedding in White* (1972), and comic vampire Count von Plasma in *Barry McKenzie Holds His Own* (1974).

John Carpenter's low-budget 1978 indie *Halloween* made the actor "a horror icon for a new and young audience,"[5] not unlike Peter Cushing and Christopher Lee—both of whom turned down the role of Michael Myers' psychiatrist, Dr. Sam Loomis, before it was offered to Pleasence. Carpenter, an "enormous fan" who considered him "one of the great character actors of all time,"[6] would subsequently cast Pleasence as the president of the United States in *Escape from New York* (1981) and Father Loomis in *Prince of Darkness* (1987).

A seemingly inevitable rash of horror movies like Dario Argento's *Phenomena* and four *Halloween* sequels notwithstanding, Pleasence found himself playing a diverse assortment of parts in his later films. Among them were a happy-go-lucky New Zealander in *Race for the Yankee Zephyr* (1981); the Israeli minister of defense in *The Ambassador* (1984); a disillusioned former military man in the Australian thriller, *Ground Zero* (1987); and a US war correspondent in Vietnam in *Dien Bien Phu* (1992).

Despite his ubiquitous presence in movies, he made no pretense about the cinema as an art form: "I make films for the money. I never, ever watch them."[7] From *Twilight Zone* ("The Changing of the Guard") and *Columbo* ("Any Old Port in a Storm") to Dennis Potter's *Blade on the Feather* and Trollope's *The Barchester Chronicles*, Pleasence's performances were often more memorable on television's small screen. Unlikely as it may seem he was originally considered for the lead in the TV sitcom *Sanford and Son* before the role was reconceived as African American—a decision to which his agent responded, "Donald could black up for the part."[8]

Pleasence never abandoned the stage, reprising *The Caretaker* under Harold Pinter's direction for a 1991 London revival. Honored with the Order of the British Empire in 1994, he was planning a production of *King Lear* with daughters Angela, Polly Jo, and Miranda when he underwent surgery for a heart valve replacement that December; though the operation was deemed successful, he died unexpectedly of complications February 2, 1995, at his home in St. Paul de Vence in the south of France. He was survived by his fourth wife, Linda, and his five daughters.

The *Independent* (London) memorialized him in their obituary as "odd man out: master of low cunning and of sinister poise, a threat to anyone's peace of mind, his own as often as not."[9] Ulli Lommel, who directed him in *The Devonsville Terror*, observed, "He was an angel to direct. He was always sweet and caring and always so sincere and quiet. . . . No matter whether he played the everyday man or an accountant or a bastard or a vicious villain, Donald was unbeatable. There was always a special tenderness, some special type of humanity that came shining through."[10]

Françoise Dorléac

The great irony of Catherine Deneuve's career is that her older sister, Françoise, was the one who wanted to be an actress, a star—not her—and that Deneuve has continued to perform for seven decades since her film debut in her teens, while Dorléac died an untimely death at the age of 25.

"People who worked with her felt Françoise was very special, like a mixture of Kate Hepburn and Kay Kendall (the late British comedienne)," Deneuve noted in a memoir. "You know, it's very strange, the people who knew her, they still talk about her."[11]

As Dorléac's career progressed, "I find that with each picture, I become more insecure, less confident about my ability to do good work. Perhaps it is because when you are younger, you don't realize what is involved in acting, how difficult a role can be,"[12] she told a magazine writer. "It's funny. The more one succeeds, the more you're hated. I feel all alone."[13]

In addition to *Cul-de-Sac*, the opportunities that came her way about the same time included costarring roles in the largely fictionalized epic *Genghis Khan* (1965), as the wife of the title character played by Omar Sharif—during which she learned to speak English—and *Where the Spies Are* (1966) with David Niven. She also played the lead in the 1967 TV movie *Julie de Chaverny Ou La double méprise*, a woman who died of love.

"Françoise wanted to know everything. In theater, she wanted to play tragedies, but she was also very tragic in life, very attuned to situations and extreme feelings," said Deneuve in retrospect. "She dreamed of having children because the idea appealed to her, but it was probably not a priority . . . She had other passions, other ambitions."[14]

Among her amours were François Truffaut and actor-dancer Jean-Pierre Cassel, her costar in *The Dance*, with whom she had a long but fruitless engagement. "I fall in love quickly, then fall out of love just as rapidly,"[15] explained Dorléac. "This is a girl who has always had a complicated personal life," observed Deneuve. "We all need to be loved, that's true. But for her, it was a vital necessity . . . That did not mean she wanted to live a love story with all the men she seduced."[16]

Though she never married because "I want to be loved without compromises,"[17] Dorléac was once asked by a journalist if she'd expect a spouse to be jealous of her doing a nude scene. "He'd better be," she responded. "If I had a husband who didn't display jealousy, I'd leave him. Then he'd be forced to go to the movie house and pay to see me nude like everyone else."[18]

Dorléac's penultimate film was Jacques Demy's *The Young Girls of Rochefort* (*Les Demoiselles de Rochefort*), a musical in which she and Catherine costarred as Solange and Delphine, twin sisters looking for love. "We were like unidentical twins, complementary but very different at the same time . . . like day and night," said Deneuve. "The Demy film allowed us to find ourselves."[19]

Tragically, on June 26, 1967, Dorléac was driving at high speed on the rain-splattered A8 Estérel-Côte d'Azur motorway en route to Nice airport when she hit the brakes, skidded. and smashed into an embankment—or a cement signpost, according to varying news reports. The Renault rental car flipped over and burst into flames. A passing motorist who witnessed the accident watched helplessly as she struggled to free herself and then burned to death in the wreckage along with her beloved pet Chihuahua.

"I fear the end, I'm afraid of death,"[20] Dorléac had ironically told a journalist in a recent joint interview with her sister. Deneuve, who had vacationed with Dorléac in St. Tropez just prior to the accident, was so devastated she was unable to talk about the tragedy for nearly 30 years. "Françoise, she is really part of a promise, a promise time did not let her accomplish. I think the excitement one experiences for her today has a lot to do with the fact that she was on the point of blossoming; she was approaching what she might have become and nobody is capable of imagining that,"[21] she stated in her 1996 memoir, *Elle s'appelait Françoise.*

The Young Girls of Rochefort would be posthumously released, along with Ken Russell's *Billion Dollar Brain*. An actress would be hired to finish dubbing her role in postproduction on the latter, yet another James Bond-style spy thriller in which she costarred with Michael Caine.

François Truffaut's tribute to the star of *The Soft Skin* would be widely quoted: "For everyone who knew her, Françoise Dorléac represented a person one rarely meets in life, a young woman incomparable in her charm, her femininity, her intelligence, her grace and her unbelievable moral force which rendered her unforgettable to anyone who spoke with her for one hour. . . . in my opinion Françoise Dorléac certainly would have found in her thirties real contact with the public who would have adored her the way those who had the chance to work with her."[22]

Lionel Stander

"With Lionel and his exuberant geyser of reminiscence, you can never be sure," observed Helen Lawrenson in her voluminous *Esquire* profile of the actor in 1967. "Just as you decide he's the biggest blatherskite since Baron Munchausen, you unexpectedly discover that some tale you thought patently a whopper turns out to be fact, not fancy."[23]

The statement was not always true, however. Though Stander frequently asserted in interviews he enjoyed success on Wall Street during the blacklist era, his daughter, Bella, set the record straight: "All that stuff about him being a stockbroker, and earning 'enough money to support myself in the style I was accustomed to,' that's a crock of shit. No. He borrowed money from family and friends and never paid it back. He sold junk bonds people bought because they felt sorry for him."[24]

The actor busied himself with a more common stock—summer stock—including revivals of *Born Yesterday* (the Broadway production of which he had turned down, thinking nothing would come of it) and *Finian's Rainbow*. He coproduced a nightclub revue with blacklisted songwriter Jay Gorney and costarred as Fluther Good in an off-Broadway production of Sean O'Casey's *The Plough and the Stars* to good notices.

The musical version of Preston Sturges' *Hail the Conquering Hero* was one of many disappointments during the blacklist era. The show, which brought Stander back to Broadway early in 1961, boasted a book by Larry Gelbart but failed to measure up to Sturges' brilliant blend of screwball comedy and social commentary. The actor was heard but not seen as the narrator of the low-budget film noir *Blast of Silence* the same year.

An offbeat, independent film called *The Moving Finger* (1963) found Stander in front of the cameras for the first time in a dozen years. Director Larry Moyer financed the avant-garde movie—about a jewel thief who takes refuge with Greenwich Village beatniks—by issuing stock, much of it to the cast themselves.

In all, it took the storm 24 years to blow over, but once the curse of the blacklist had been removed, Stander made up for it with a vengeance. His performance in *Cul-de-Sac*, crowned by a standing ovation at the Berlin Film Festival, opened the floodgates; cast as a barman in Sergio Leone's *Once Upon a Time in the West*, he found himself in great demand in Italy and became the unofficial mayor of Rome's Via Veneto.

One of his more unusual pictures was Andrzej Wajda's *Gates to Paradise*, a film about the 13th-century children's crusade shot in Yugoslavia, in which he played a monk. Among Stander's later English-language films were *Pulp* with Michael Caine, *Treasure Island* with Orson Welles, *The Black Bird* (a parody of *The Maltese Falcon*), Martin Scorsese's *New York, New York* (as Liza Minnelli's agent), and Steven Spielberg's *1941*.

The enduring popularity of Sidney Sheldon's 1979–1984 TV series *Hart to Hart*, featuring Stander as Max the majordomo, fueled more than 100 episodes and a succession of TV movies. He completed work on a fifth TV movie just weeks before his death from lung cancer, November 30, 1994, at the age of 86. He was survived by his sixth wife, Stephana, and six daughters.

Character actor Allen Garfield, who portrayed Stander on stage in Eric Bentley's blacklist docudrama, *Are You Now or Have You Ever Been . . .* , suggested he was "deserving of a posthumous honorary Oscar for his lifetime of achievement and for the dignity and honor he bestowed on the film industry, both on-screen as an actor and off-screen going head to head with HUAC."[25]

"Not only did he not inform on anybody, he didn't equivocate, didn't take the Fifth Amendment, and didn't pretend not to remember anything," his *Hart to Hart* costar, Robert J. Wagner, recalled in admiration. "As far as Lionel was concerned, his politics were nobody's damn business, period. . . . He was a very tough-minded man and firm in his convictions, which remained proudly left-wing."[26]

Jack MacGowran

MacGowran labored long and hard on *Dance of the Vampires*, a rare starring role slated for 10 weeks filming that took 20 to complete. In the evenings he rehearsed for a Dublin production of O'Casey's *Juno and the Paycock*, a characterization of Joxer Daly that would win acclaim for "a terrifyingly powerful performance."[27] Though he should have taken a much needed break, he then traveled to Spain to play clown-soldier Private Juniper in Richard Lester's surreal anti-war comedy, *How I Won the War*; when the film wrapped, however, he was hospitalized for fatigue and nervous exhaustion.

There would be other film roles—including a star turn as an absent-minded entomologist in *Wonderwall* (dreamed up by Gérard Brach) and decent supporting parts in *Age of Consent* with his friend James Mason (as the star's ne'er-do-well buddy), Peter Brooks' *King Lear* (as the Fool, opposite Paul Scofield), and *The Exorcist*—but the remainder of his career would be devoted primarily to his one-man show based on the works of Samuel Beckett.

When the performer first compiled an anthology from the writer's work, Beckett was less than wholly satisfied. In its final shape and form, however, *Beginning to End* achieved a harmony rarely present in a one-man show. By the time actor and author reunited in Paris in 1970 to resurrect the monodrama and restructure it into its final form, Beckett had won the Nobel Prize for Literature. *Beginning to End* was comprised of Beckett's poems, passages from the novels, and excerpts from the plays and now had a central theme: "the story of a man's innermost thoughts on the statement that he's going to die."[28]

MacGowran was intimately acquainted with the characters who peopled Beckett's novels and plays. As a reformed alcoholic and a manic depressive, he identified with their dark souls in a way few other actors could. He recognized their black Irish humor because he had grown up with it; he knew their hopelessness because he had lived it. But he also sensed the affirmation of life at the core of Beckett's work that had eluded others.

MacGowran changed forever the public perception of Beckett, from a purveyor of gloom and despair to a writer of wit and humanity. It was not an intellectual rapport they had but a spiritual affinity. Where critics and scholars were preoccupied by the nihilism, MacGowran was aroused by the writer's comic imagery, his courage, and above all, his compassion for the human condition.

"No matter how you approach Beckett, through his novels or his plays, no matter what setting he places his characters in for dramatic purposes, never will they give way to despair," observed MacGowran. "The key word in all his plays is 'perhaps' . . . and therein lies the hope that there's a fifty-fifty chance of things going our way."[29] When MacGowran asked the author how much laughter he expected from the show, the answer came readily: "As much as you can get."[30] As the actor said once in disbelief: "People find Beckett morose. I find him so funny."[31]

The playwright himself directed the show, dedicating himself as fully to the task as he had to the creation of the words themselves; true to form, he refused to take any credit for it. As per his custom, however, he was nowhere to be seen when *Beginning to End* opened in Paris in 1970. Instead, he waited backstage with a warm embrace for his confrere. As usual, words between them were few. "Jack was like a brother," Beckett said later. "I didn't have to talk to him; I didn't have to direct him. He just knew."[32]

The actor traveled to New York that fall to portray the title role in Gurney Campbell's *Gandhi*, which opened and closed on the same night. Little did the actor dream the biggest fiasco of his long and erratic life in the theatre would make possible his crowning achievement, the presentation of his solo show under the auspices of the New York Shakespeare Festival.

The actor was afraid Beckett might be a writer of limited appeal in the United States, still a bit ahead of his time, but Joseph Papp convinced him otherwise. Neither were prepared for the success that greeted the anthology, particularly the Obie award for Best Actor in an Off-Broadway performance. "Author and actor are so commonly rooted in spirit that if Beckett were an actor he would be MacGowran, if MacGowran were a writer he would be Beckett," observed Mel Gussow in the *New York Times*. "It is an evening in the presence of two consummate artists exactly in tune with each other."[33]

The US tour that followed was a triumph on paper but a washout financially, like all of his artistic successes. What kept him going above all else was an insatiable appetite for Beckett on the part of college students. "They know what I'm doing," he enthused, "though I can't stand the intellectuals who come backstage and drive me batty looking for meanings in Beckett that simply do not exist."[34]

The actor was midway through an off-Broadway production of O'Casey's *The Plough and the Stars*—in which he played the mock-heroic Fluther Good to rave reviews—when friends and associates noticed a decline in him. MacGowran had a spectacular career ahead of him when he succumbed on January 30, 1973, at age 54. Death was widely attributed to the London flu, but the cause was an angina condition he had sought to ignore. He was survived by his wife, Gloria, and his daughter Tara, who went on to become an actress (notably in *Secret Places*) and producer.

"It was a most unexpected death. I just could not believe it when I heard. . . . he could take tremendous endurance. You could not exhaust that man,"[35] said Roman Polanski.

"Jack's stage presence stays with me more than anything . . . this frail thing with this enormous power. He walked a tightrope as if it were a three-lane highway," said Peter O'Toole. "Jack was one of the few if not the only Irishman who broke out of 'Irishry' without losing his root, his Irish strength. He was the only actor in my generation who fought it and won."[36]

The Supporting Cast

William Franklyn (Cecil) went on to become host of ITV's *The Masterspy*, the voice of the Book on Radio 4's *The Hitchhiker's Guide to the Galaxy* (replacing Peter Jones), Lord Mountbatten in the TV movie *Diana: Her True Story*, and a busy pitchman on TV commercials.

Robert Dorning (Fairweather) appeared in TV's *Dad's Army* and *Coronation Street*. His later films included *The Human Factor*, *Ragtime*, *Evil Under the Sun*, Polanski's *Pirates*, and *Mona Lisa*. His daughter Stacey starred in the TV series *The Adventures of Black Beauty*.

Marie Kean (Marion Fairweather) followed *Cul-de-Sac* with the Dublin revival of Sean O'Casey's *Juno and the Paycock* with Jack MacGowran and her friend Peter O'Toole; in the 1970s she joined the Royal Shakespeare Company at Stratford, and starred in the title role of John B. Keane's *Big Maggie* in its world premiere at the Cork Opera House. She also toured in her one-woman show about literary Dublin, *Soft Morning City*. Among Kean's noteworthy film appearances were David Lean's *Ryan's Daughter*, Stanley Kubrick's *Barry Lyndon* (as the title character's mother), and John Huston's *The Dead*.

Renée Houston (Christopher's mother) went on to appear in TV's *River Rivals* and make guest appearances in several series, including *Doctor in the House*. Her later films included *The Spy with a Cold Nose*, *Carry On at Your Convenience*, and *Legend of the Werewolf*.

Geoffrey Sumner (Christopher's father) appeared in such films as *That's Your Funeral* and *There Goes the Bride*, along with TV's *Emergency Ward 10* and *The Reluctant Romeo*; his later stage efforts took him to New York City and South Africa.

Iain Quarrier (Christopher) would become perhaps best known as the gay vampire in pursuit of Roman Polanski himself in *Dance of the Vampires*. Following his appearance as a fashion model in *Wonderwall*, he coproduced Jean-Luc Godard's *One Plus One* (also known as *Sympathy for the Devil*), featuring the Rolling Stones. Godard urged the audience to walk out at the film's London premiere, accusing the producers of ruining the film, and punched Quarrier in the face. The actor was reportedly invited by Sharon Tate to her Los Angeles home on the fateful night of her murder in 1969 but was delayed making a film in the California desert. He then disappeared from public view, turning up decades later in London, destitute and mentally ill, at the center of a series of bizarre, headline-making incidents.

Jacqueline Bisset (Jacqueline) was at the outset of a career that has lasted seven decades when she appeared in *Cul-de-Sac*. She followed up small roles in films like *Two for the Road* and *Bullitt* with François Truffaut's *Day for Night*, *The Deep*, *Rich and Famous* (which she coproduced, sans credit), and John Huston's *Under the Volcano*. Bisset has since been seen in such television mini-series as *Napoleon and Josephine: A Love Story* (as Josephine), *Joan of Arc* (which garnered her a Primetime Emmy nomination), and *Dancing on the Edge* (earning a Golden Globe award for her role as Lady Cremone); TV series include *Nip/Tuck*, *Rizzoli and Isles*, and *Counterpart*.

Trevor Delaney (Horace) appeared unbilled in *The Family Way* and *The Anniversary*. His career ended abruptly when his parents divorced. The former child actor is now a general manager for a consultancy firm in Australia.

Gérard Brach, Co-Screenwriter

A man of mystery, Brach was something of an enigma by circumstance if not by design. Stricken with agoraphobia, the writer rarely ventured past the door of his apartment. "In fact, if you don't know someone in his inner circle . . . You'll never find him," observed a reporter for the *Los Angeles Times*, who concluded on meeting the casually dressed writer, "he looks more like a prosperous businessman from Cleveland than the elusive legend of French film that he is."[37]

In time Brach's prolific collaboration with Polanski would total nine features for the director, including *Repulsion, Dance of the Vampires, What?, The Tenant, Tess, Pirates, Frantic,* and *Bitter Moon*—not to mention Jean-Daniel Simon's *The Girl Across the Way* (1968), Brach's own *The Boat on the Grass* (1971), and an unproduced version of *Cinderella.*

"I learned cinema by being Polanski's friend and by working with him a great deal . . . he taught me everything he knew," Brach told a journalist. "We are very different in the way we work but I have total rapport with him in terms of ideas."[38] As Polanski explained to *Positif:* "There's no real method. It's more that we've developed a kind of routine. I explain the theme and we discuss it together, then steadily improve on things. Little by little a sequence is created which seems worth putting to paper, and that's when Gérard starts to write."[39]

The writer also enjoyed noteworthy multiple-film collaborations with Claude Berri (*The Two of Us*, the BAFTA Award-winning Marcel Pagnol adaptation *Jean de Florette* and its sequel *Manon des Sources*); Jean-Jacques Annaud (*Quest for Fire, The Name of the Rose, The Bear,* and others); and Andrei Konchalovsky (*Maria's Lovers* and *Shy People*). In addition, he scripted *Identification of a Woman* for Michelangelo Antonioni.

Brach and Annaud found an immediate rapport, deciding to adapt *Quest for Fire* from J. H. Rosny's book of the same name on the day they met. "He allowed me to make films with images that had filled my imagination since my youth, images of adventures, dreams, open spaces," said Brach, who took a nonverbal approach to the story. "He is a perfectionist. We can tackle any subject and he accepts ideas that bring nature into play."[40]

Gil Taylor, Cinematographer

Polanski and Taylor "had a lot of arguments and fights"[41] during *Cul-de-Sac*. The duo eventually patched things up after meeting in a bar and reteamed satisfactorily on *Macbeth*. During a career that lasted more than 65 years, the cinematographer filmed several episodes of TV's *The Avengers*, *2001: A Space Odyssey* (additional photography), Richard Donner's *The Omen*, *Meetings with Remarkable Men* for Peter Brook, and John Badham's *Dracula*.

He had to practically drag Alfred Hitchcock—who "never looked through the camera" and "had no interest in setups"[42]—to view rushes on *Frenzy*. He butted heads with George Lucas over the visual style of the first *Star Wars*; he nearly quit to defend his point of view and decided when it was over, "I wouldn't do another film with him for anything."[43]

Taylor continued filming commercials after he retired to the Isle of Wight to paint landscapes and run a dairy farm. He earned the British Society of Cinematographers (BSC) best cinematography award for *The Omen,* and the BSC lifetime achievement award in 2001. Though he never worked in Hollywood, he spoke of his respect for Gregg Toland (*Citizen Kane*) and others when the American Society of Cinematographers honored him with its International Achievement Award in 2006.

"He had a great appetite for life, and I think it's no accident that he connected with directors of humor,"[44] director Curtis Hanson observed of Taylor. "He's a very funny guy, and I think that gives him a sensibility to come at scenes in a little different manner." Recalled Richard Donner, "He took me down some interesting roads. And he taught me a lot about the motivations of cameras—that you don't just move a camera arbitrarily. But it was never a lecture. He was just wonderful." After Donner recommended Taylor to George Lucas for *Star Wars* and things were less than wonderful, he would get phone calls:

"Gil would call me and say, 'What did you do to me? This is a crazy movie, and these are crazy filmmakers who don't understand me!' And I'd say, 'Gil, you better get used to it, because this is the future.'"[45]

Gene Gutowski, Producer

Gutowski denied his Jewish origins, "creating a duality of existence which I have maintained for most of my life,"[46] as he noted in his memoirs. More than half a century later he relived the past as coproducer of Polanski's film *The Pianist*—resuming his partnership with the director after a hiatus of some three decades—though the two had never discussed the Holocaust. For Gutowski, the Oscar- and Palme d'Or-winning picture was "a personal catharsis" and "in many ways the crowning moment of my life."[47] (His mother, who perished in the death camp at Belzec, had been a concert pianist.)

Gutowski also produced Simon Hesera's *A Day at the Beach* (written but not coproduced by Polanski, despite credit to the contrary), Jerzy Skolimowski's *The Adventures of Gerard* (cowritten by Gutowski, based on stories by Sir Arthur Conan Doyle), and Abraham Polonsky's *Romance of a Horsethief.*

"It would appear that throughout my entire life circumstances often beyond my control, or even pure chance, have always placed me at the right moment in time at precisely the right place, allowing me to survive and often succeed," observed Gutowski. "In the end, fate has allowed me to bear witness to the tumultuous history of most of the twentieth century and even, on occasion, to play a small part in it."[48]

Krzysztof Komeda, Music

After embellishing his résumé with *Dance of the Vampires* and *Rosemary's Baby* for Polanski, Komeda scored Jerzy Skolimowski's

Barrier and *The Departure,* and Buzz Kulik's *Riot.* "We'd talk about his music, because journalists would ask him what kind of music he played," Polanski recalled. "They'd ask, 'How would you describe your music?' And he'd say, 'It's film music.' And he was right. He brought a different perspective to a film. He didn't try to sell his music regardless of whether it suited the film or not. He'd really bring a certain quality to a film."[49]

Though there is some discrepancy surrounding Komeda's tragic, early death in 1969, he apparently fell and seriously injured himself on a walk in the Hollywood Hills, after a late-night drinking binge with writer friend Marek Hłasko. After Hłasko picked him up, then stumbled and dropped him—according to Polanski—he sustained further injury. He developed a blood clot on the brain, requiring emergency surgery, but lapsed into a coma without regaining consciousness; he died shortly after his wife flew him back to Warsaw.

Astigmatic, an album recorded by the Komeda Quintet in 1965, has been called "One of the great jazz records of its time"[50] by *New York Times* critic Ben Ratliff. London-based music reviewer Stuart Nicholson asserted the album "has become a bellwether for European jazz [that] represents a fresh approach and a different way of hearing and playing jazz."[51] Komeda's unique sound, influenced by Slavic lyricism and 19th-century Polish romantic music tradition, is influential to this day.

Alastair McIntyre, Editor

McIntyre went on to cut six films directed by Polanski in all, including *Macbeth, What?,* and *Tess.* Michael Klinger would recall him as "a very capable man, but Roman's slave."[52] He also served as editor on *My Side of the Mountain* and Jerzy Skolimowski's *The Adventures of Gerard.*

Voytek, Production Designer

Following *Cul-de-Sac* Voytek designed *The Man in the Glass Booth* with his old friend Donald Pleasence for its world premiere in London; he worked extensively in television as a designer and director, receiving two BAFTA Awards for his design work. The Voytek Collection is housed in the Victoria and Albert Museum.

Michael Klinger and Tony Tenser, Presenters

Gaining respectability with *Repulsion* and *Cul-de-Sac*, Klinger and Tenser split up to go their own separate ways shortly after the latter. Klinger went on to produce *Get Carter* and *Pulp* (both with Michael Caine), and *Gold* and *Shout at the Devil* (both with Roger Moore). Tenser specialized in horror films, notably *Witchfinder General* with Vincent Price; other efforts included *Hannie Caulder* with Raquel Welch.

Sam Waynberg, Executive Producer

Waynberg produced or coproduced Andrzej Wajda's *Gates to Paradise*, the concert documentary *Stamping Ground*, R. W. Fassbinder's *Querelle*, and the French crime drama *Un dimanche de flic* over the course of his career, along with several movies in the Israeli *Lemon Popsicle* series.

EPILOGUE

Dance of the Vampires was a parody of Hammer horror films on one level and a knockabout farce recalling the heyday of Mack Sennett and the Keystone Cops on another. It was a decided change of pace for Polanski, who would act a prominent role and fall in love with leading lady Sharon Tate, whom he would marry early in 1968. "I think he put more of himself into [*Vampires*] than into any other film," asserted cinematographer Douglas Slocombe. "The figure of Alfred [played by Polanski] is very much like Roman himself—a slight figure, young and a little defenseless—a touch of Kafka. It is very much a personal statement of his own humor."[1]

Taking an "instant dislike" to Polanski, producer William Castle had no intention of letting him direct *Rosemary's Baby*, for which he'd snapped up the rights after Alfred Hitchcock passed on it. Despite the young filmmaker's cockiness, however, Castle found him "fascinating, brilliant and wonderfully receptive,"[2] with such an intelligent take on how to handle the material, he changed his mind. Studio head Robert Evans was sold from the beginning: "This was a talent. He could make you jump out of your skin."[3] Ira Levin's story of a young woman who is impregnated by Satan and surrounded by devil-worshipping witches earned the director a bigger paycheck—$150,000—than all his previous films combined, while his screenplay would garner an Oscar nomination. Reviewers recommended it "only for mature audiences with strong stomachs"[4] and Polanski was attacked by Catholics. "Never by witches" though, said the director. "Witches told me they liked the film."[5]

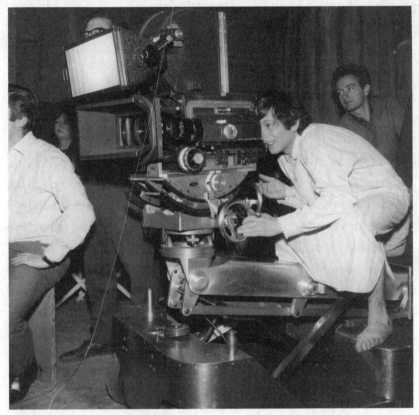

Polanski behind the camera on Dance of the Vampires, *still costumed for his role in the film.* MGM/PHOTOFEST

Witchcraft and occult rituals would resurface—to Polanski's shock and astonishment—when the media chronicled the savage slayings of his wife and friends in 1969. "The reporting about Sharon and the murders was virtually criminal," he vented to *Playboy* magazine two years later. "Reading the papers, I could not believe my eyes . . . They blamed the victims for their own murders." Legitimate publications and scandal sheets alike "all groped for 'irony' in the murders, which was nonsense, and then turned my films into a metaphor"[6] for them, in Polanski's view.

Scrapping plans to make a biographical film about composer Nic-
colo Paganini and a western about the ill-fated Donner party, the
director chose instead to return to work by tackling Shakespeare's
Macbeth. Asked what would he say to those who felt it was "a kind
of catharsis" after suffering the tragic loss of his wife and friends,
he responded, "I would say they are full of shit, because it's not so."
Defending the bloodshed in the film in pure Chekhovian terms, he
stated, "If you make a film about a murder, you have to *show* the murder, or do a film about something else." No one would ever lose their
head more realistically than Jon Finch in the title role, an impressive
feat before the advent of CGI. Making the film was not difficult, said
Polanski, "It's only later when you put it together and show it to an
audience that you realize there's something horrific in it."[7]

If his sex comedy *What?* would be largely dismissed, his follow-up
film would be widely considered his greatest accomplishment. Ralph

Polanski with Francesca Annis on the set of Macbeth. COLUMBIA PICTURES/PHOTOFEST

Bellamy, who was reportedly offered John Huston's role in *China-town* (1974), rejected it: "I was sent a script that didn't look at all like the picture when Polanski finished it. It read like a porno film."[8] The director did an uncredited rewrite of Robert Towne's script, working with the screenwriter eight weeks, eight hours a day to restructure it. Critics attacked the film for being overly violent, but there was little apart from the bloody, enigmatic ending ("Happy endings make me puke"[9]) and the scene where Polanski gave Jack Nicholson's detective a visceral warning by slicing open his nose. "I directed that scene," stated Nicholson, who had auditioned unsuccessfully for the male lead in *Rosemary's Baby*. "Every actor needs a director and when he has a good one he gives a better performance, it's as simple as that."[10]

In the title role of *The Tenant* (*Le locataire* 1976), Polanski played a transvestite as neurotic as any of his female characters. He was preparing his next film, *The First Deadly Sin*, the following year in Los Angeles when everything went off the rails. His private life became

Polanski discusses the filming of Chinatown *with John Huston and Jack Nicholson.* PARAMOUNT PICTURES/PHOTOFEST

public once again when he was arrested and subsequently plead guilty to having sex with a minor. "I like young women," he candidly acknowledged to TV interviewer Clive James. "Looking back, it was bound to happen."[11] He would end up fleeing the United States, asserting a fair trial would be impossible. The woman in question, Samantha Geimer, would later tell talk show host Larry King: "He served his time, he did everything he was asked to do. And we had a corrupt judge who was being dishonest; he had no reason to trust the system to work for him. And I've been so much more damaged by the court system and the media than by him . . . It's easy to forgive him."[12]

Endeavoring to make a great love story, Polanski chose one Sharon had brought to his attention—Thomas Hardy's late 19th-century novel, *Tess of the D'Urbervilles*—or simply *Tess*, as the director would title his adaptation starring Nastassia Kinski. "Think of all the great love stories of history. They all had sad or tragic endings. They have to end badly or there's no conflict,"[13] he told journalists at the Cannes Film Festival. The picture was released in Europe a year before it found its way to the United States late in 1980, as a result of a rave review by Charles Champlin in the *Los Angeles Times*, who called it a "nearly perfect" adaptation of the novel and noted Hardy's "resolutely pessimistic . . . view of life obviously has sharp resonances for Polanski."[14] *Le Monde* observed: "Polanski the provocateur has become Polanski the romantic."[15] The film won three Oscars.

The 1980s took Polanski all over the map, beginning with a return to the stage in Peter Shaffer's *Amadeus*. Struck by the play's theatricality, he directed himself as Mozart in Warsaw and Paris. He ended a long hiatus from the screen with the adventure comedy *Pirates* (1986), originally envisioned with Jack Nicholson in the lead but finally realized with Walter Matthau. He fared substantially better with *Frantic* (1988), a Hitchcockian thriller shot in his native Paris. While the film introduced the actress Emmanuelle Seigner into his life and work, he found time during postproduction to star in a Steven Berkoff's stage adaptation of Kafka's *Metamorphosis*.

Seigner had married Polanski by the time she returned for the sexually adventurous *Bitter Moon* (1992), which the director would find himself defending while still in production. "If it's explicit sometimes, it's for valid reasons. It's not for exploiting the public, not for commercial reasons, that it talks about sex or shows nudity," he asserted. Asked if the movie might give his enemies ammunition, given the charges against him, he responded, "Well, so be it. This is a risk I have to take. I can't be making pictures respecting the feelings of people toward me or against me as a person. I have to be the artist first."[16]

Death and the Maiden (1994), a claustrophobic three-character drama adapted from the play by Ariel Dorfman, provided a return to more familiar territory. A "grindingly creepy whodunit"[17] for one

Polanski on the set of Frantic. COURTESY OF BISON ARCHIVES/WARNER BROS.

critic, it suggested "the discipline of *Frantic* rather than the go-for-broke-excess of *Bitter Moon*"[18] for another reviewer.

Polanski declined when first approached with the idea for a stage musical based on *Dance of the Vampires*; ultimately he "convinced myself . . . it maintained the spirit of the movie"[19] and agreed to direct. *Tanz der Vampire* opened in Vienna in 1997 and became a runaway hit.

The Ninth Gate (1999), "a fairy tale for adults"[20] in which the director would dance with the devil once more, had the obvious satanic element in common with *Rosemary's Baby* but its subtle black humor went over audiences' heads. "I wanted the film to be more of a comedy, more of a parody of the genre . . . but it seems like nobody really got it."[21] Small wonder he once told a journalist: "All I say is this: don't ever ask me to explain any of my pictures."[22]

The story of a musician's struggle to survive the Holocaust would ultimately provide the filmmaker with a means to partially salvage his reputation. "I always knew that one day I would make a film about this painful chapter in Polish history, but I didn't want it to be autobiographical,"[23] Polanski said in a statement about *The Pianist* (2002). Though he initially felt Wladyslaw Szpilman's memoirs were "just one more book about the Nazi occupation,"[24] producer Gene Gutowski persuaded him to reconsider. He endeavored to "tell it the way it was . . . no more, no less,"[25] re-creating moments he remembered from his youth while relying on Szpilman's "extremely accurate" book for authentic details. The film would earn seven Oscar nominations and three awards, including a controversial one for him as director, as well as for Ronald Harwood's (*The Dresser*) screenplay adaptation, and Adrien Brody's performance as Szpilman. *The Pianist* would also win the coveted Palme d'Or at Cannes as well as BAFTA Awards for himself and the film.

The desire to make a picture his young children—Morgane and Elvis, eleven and six at the time—could identify with led Polanski to film Dickens' *Oliver Twist* (2005). The echoes of his own child-hood, scrounging and scavenging for a living after escaping from the ghetto, are unmistakable in his depiction of the impoverished orphan. Ben Kingsley, who played Fagin, expressed admiration for "what Roman does with his extraordinary knowledge of European turmoil and his acquaintance with childhood and death hand in hand . . . [the way] he uses his traumatized soul as a child."[26]

The Raymond Chandler-like story of *The Ghost Writer* (also known as *The Ghost*, 2010) found Polanski making a Kafkaesque thriller once more, with unexpected real-life resonance. Pierce Bros-nan's disgraced politician, tarnished by scandal and hounded by the media, aroused in the director "a lot of sympathy for my charac-ters."[27] He was forced to complete the editing in prison after an arrest in Switzerland relating to his 1977 conviction.

The claustrophobia of *Carnage* (2011), Polanski's filmization of Yasmina Reza's "comedy of bad manners," *God of Carnage*, had crit-ics reaching for comparisons to the confined spaces of everything from *Repulsion* to *Death and the Maiden*; as one concluded, "he's back to scorched-earth warfare waged indoors."[28] The same could be said of *Venus in Fur* (*La Vénus à la fourrure*, 2014), a two-character sexual power play between a stage director and an actress audition-ing for a role, adapted from a play by David Ives. The playwright, who cowrote the short-lived Broadway musical version of *Dance of the Vampires*, gave the director a rave review. "His command of the nuances of English dialogue was amazing—he saw how lines could be better and sharper," said Ives, who got a frantic call from Polanski at one point asking for permission to move a stage direction from one page of the script to another. "That is the level of detail he oper-ates on. But I didn't mind. For me, it was heaven."[29]

Based on a True Story (*D'après une histoire vraie*, 2017), yet another two-character drama adapted from a French novel, would be nega-tively compared by critics with *The Ghost Writer* and other thrillers such as Stephen King's *Misery*. Some reviewers took offense to *An Officer and a Spy* (*J'accuse*, 2019), Polanski's hard-wrought film about the notorious scandal surrounding Alfred Dreyfus, a Jewish officer wrongfully convicted for treason, court-martialed, and imprisoned. Others lauded the historical drama, like Phil de Semlyen of *Time Out*: "It's going too far to say that it looks like an Auguste Renoir painting and plays like a Jean Renoir movie," he wrote, "but not by much."[30]

As Tim Grierson summed up the controversy in *Screen*: "There will be a temptation to ascribe certain motivations to Polanski's decision to film a movie about a horrible miscarriage of justice. But, interestingly, from the evidence on screen . . . the director seems fairly wary about how liberating exoneration truly is."[31] The film swept the awards at the Venice Film Festival and won César Awards, the French Oscars, for best director and best adapted screenplay (cowritten with Robert Harris, who also collaborated with Polanski on *The Ghost Writer*).

The director had long wanted to make a film about the Dreyfus Affair. "The story of a man unfairly accused is always fascinating, but it is also very much a current issue, given the upsurge in anti-Semitism," stated Polanski. Not only did he relate personally to moments in the film, "I can see the same determination to deny the facts and condemn me for things I have not done. Most of the people who harass me do not know me and know nothing about the case."[32]

Oscar-winning actor Jean Dujardin, who costarred in *An Officer and a Spy*, had high praise for Polanski when asked about working with him. "He is a filmmaker who demands from others the same extreme precision he requires from himself," said Dujardin. "Roman is a man who studied fine arts: he sets up his shots just like paintings. Every detail needs to be perfect. . . . Roman is a complex and demanding person who won't let anything deflect him from his path.

He has to see the project through to the end. He needs to go out and find the truth."[33]

When asked about retirement in the recent past, the auteur told a *Variety* reporter, "I never really imagined how one can retire. . . . I think the best moments in my life are when I work. It was my passion when I was a young man, and it remains my passion. I feel probably the way a carpenter feels when he's making a beautiful chair and seeing the result of his work. The work itself is satisfying, the process of getting the result."[34]

CLOSING CREDITS

CUL-DE-SAC: CREDITED ONSCREEN

Cast

Donald Pleasence	George
Françoise Dorléac	Teresa
Lionel Stander	Richard
Jack MacGowran	Albie
William Franklyn	Cecil
Robert Dorning	Philip Fairweather
Marie Kean	Marion Fairweather
Renée Houston	Christopher's mother
Geoffrey Sumner	Christopher's father
Iain Quarrier	Christopher
Jackie Bisset	Jacqueline
Trevor Delaney	Horace [a.k.a. Nicholas]

Crew

Roman Polanski	Director
Roman Polanski and Gérard Brach	Original Screenplay
John Sutro	Translation
Ted Sturgis, Roger Simons	First Assistant Directors
Gilbert Taylor, BSC	Director of Photography
Geoffrey Seaholme, Roy Ford	Camera Operators

George Stephenson	Sound Mixer
Dee Vaughan	Continuity
Laurie Turner	Stills [photography]
David Campling	Sound Editor
Maude Spector	Casting
Alan Brownie	Make-up
Joyce James	Hairdresser
Bridget Sellers	Wardrobe
Stephen Dalby	Sound Supervisor [honorary credit]
Gerry Humphries	Dubbing Mixer
Alf Pegley	Props
Bowie Films Ltd. [Les Bowie]	Special Effects
Don Weeks	Production Manager
Terry Glinwood	Production Controller
George Lack	Art Director
Voytek	Production Designer
Alastair McIntyre	Editor
Robert Sterne	Production Supervisor
Komeda	Music
Sam Waynberg	Executive Producer
Gene Gutowski	Producer

CUL-DE-SAC: UNCREDITED

Richard Harrison, Stand-In for Donald Pleasence
Frankie Tomsett, Stand-In for Françoise Dorléac
Jock Taylor, Stand-In for Lionel Stander
Richard Harrison, Stand-In for Jack MacGowran
Jock Taylor, Stand-In for Robert Dorning
Roman Polanski, Double for Lionel Stander (hands)
Gérard Brach, Double for Jack MacGowran (corpse)

Dee Vaughan, Voiceover for Telephone Operator [probable]
Roman Polanski, Voiceover for Seagull
Alexandra Stewart, Teresa (preproduction rehearsals)
Michael Klinger and Tony Tenser, Presenters (financiers)
Hercules Bellville, Runner
Jim Darling, Construction Crew
Denton Scott, Cashier
Valerie Kent, Production Secretary
George Bicknell, Chief Electrician
Bert Mortimer, Electrician
Reg Keywood, Carpenter
Dick Hyde, Stag
Alf Cornwall, Rigger
Richard Furness, Painter
Bill Parker, Props
Robin O'Donoghue, Sound Camera Operator
Jim Powell, Generator Operator
Dodger Norris, Camera Car Operator
Reg Everest, Painters Lab
Frank Gell, Clapper/Loader
Ken Reynolds, Sound Boom Operator
Roy Mingaye, Sound Maintenance
John Ireland, Electrician
Hamid Ali, Electrician
John Winter, Electrician
Claude Carlton, Props
Dickie Gill, Transportation
Jimmy Patterson, Driver
Jack Taylor, Driver
Tommy Brooker, Grip
Jan Lenica, Title Designer; Poster Art/Design
Gilbert Wood, Scenic Artist

Stuart A. Black, Second Assistant Director
Terry Schubert, Special Effects Assistant
Stanley Long, Location Scouting Pilot
Mrs. Bill, Unit Nurse
Lily Poyser, Publicist
Erich Mehl, Financier
David Bailey, Stills (pressbook photography)
Graham Whitworth, Director of Publicity for Compton
Alan Kean, Managing Director of Distribution for Compton
Martin Ransohoff, Re-edit for US Distribution [unauthorized]
Film Finances Ltd., Completion Bond
Compton-Tekli Film Productions
Compton Film Distributors/Compton-Cameo, UK Distribution
Sigma III/Filmways, US Distribution

Note: The Call Sheets (courtesy of Roman Polanski) and Movement Order (courtesy of Roger Simons) are the primary sources for the Uncredited.

ACKNOWLEDGMENTS

First and foremost, I am indebted to Roman Polanski, and to his secretary at R. P. Productions, Françoise Piraud, for sharing the shooting script of *Cul-de-Sac* and production call sheets, not to mention his taking time from a busy schedule for the interview that began our acquaintance long ago.

I am grateful to Roman's US agent, Jeff Berg, for setting the wheels in motion; and for making it happen, my editors at Applause Theatre & Cinema Books, Chris Chappell, Laurel Myers, Barbara Claire, and John Cerullo; and my agent, Charlotte Gusay of Charlotte Gusay Literary Agency.

For interviews and conversations, I'm obliged to Trevor Delaney, Gene Gutowski, Fionnuala Kenny, Tony Klinger, Gloria MacGowran, Jack MacGowran, Robin O'Donoghue, Donald Pleasence, Roger Simons, Bella Stander, and Lionel Stander.

Special thanks to Ron Karlson for his erudite translations; Ewa Mazierska for her splendid introduction; Christopher Weedman for additional research; and Marc Wanamaker of Bison Archives for images. Thanks are due also to Anthony Balducci, Cindy Burkhardt, Ivan Butler, Ian Caunce, Charlie Christ, Gary Claussen, Hilton Edwards, Glenn Erickson, Concepta Fennell, Heidi Fitzgerald, Sam Gill, Christopher Gullo, Michael J. Hayde, Marek Hendrykowski, Dieter Hofmann, Victoria Jiménez, Keith M. Johnston, Marie Kean, Tara MacGowran, Joseph McBride, James McNeff, Glenn Mitchell,

Eric Myers, James L. Neibaur, Mel Neuhaus, Jack Nicholson, Marek Nizich-Nizinski, Peter O'Toole, Angela Pleasence, Joe Roman, Keith Scott, Mike Siegel, Tony Sloman, David Sterritt, Muriel Wagner, and Bob Weiskopf.

Additionally, I thank the Academy of Motion Picture Arts and Sciences, Margaret Herrick Library, Rachel Bernstein and staff; Alamy Ltd.; *American Cinematographer*, David E. Williams; BFI National Film Archive, British Film Institute, Nigel Good and staff; Blue Underground Ltd.; Broadcasting, Entertainment, Cinematograph and Theatre Union (BECTU); Cannon Films; *Cineaste*; Cinémathèque française, Bibliothèque du film and staff; Columbia Pictures; Compton Films; Constantin Film; The Criterion Collection, Karen Stetler; Donald Pleasence Appreciation Society; Film Art Gallery; Françoise Dorléac-Goddess of the New Wave; Granger Historical Picture Archive; *Guardian*; *Independent*; Janus Films; Larry Edmunds Bookshop; *L'Avant-Scène Cinema*; *Le Monde*; lindisfarne.org.uk; *Los Angeles Times*; Metro-Goldwyn-Mayer Studios, Inc.; William Morrow & Co.; The Movie Poster Page; mptvimages.com; National Trust, Lindisfarne-Castle, Holy Island, Nick Lewis; New York Public Library for the Performing Arts, Lincoln Center, Billy Rose Theatre Collection, Steve Massa; *New York Times*; *New York World Journal Tribune*; Newport Beach Public Library; newspapers.com; Nordic Posters; Orange Public Library; Paramount Pictures; PBS/KCET Public Television; Photofest; Republic Pictures; Selznick International Pictures; *Screen International*; Shutterstock; Sigma III; Sony Columbia; Twentieth Century-Fox; United Artists; University of California, Berkeley Art Museum & Pacific Film Archive; University of Mississippi Press; University of Southern California, Cinema-Television Library, Doheny Library, Ned Comstock; University of Texas at Austin, Harry Ransom Center; *Variety*; Victoria and Albert Museum, London; Warner Bros.; *Washington Post*; Wikipedia Commons.

NOTES

PROLOGUE

1. Fred Hauptfuhrer, "Roman Polanski, Long Stalked by Tragedy, Is Booked in a Sex-and-Drug Whodunit," *People*, March 28, 1977.

2. Tuska, "Roman Polanski," 405.

3. "Clive James Meets Roman Polanski," *London Weekend Television*, 1984.

4. Tuska, "Roman Polanski," 379.

5. Michael Delahaye and Jean-André Fieschi, "Landscape of a Mind," *Cahiers du Cinema in English*, no. 3, February 1966, reprinted in Polanski, *Three Film Scripts*, 208–9.

6. Greenberg, *A Retrospective*, 14.

7. Ibid.

8. Polanski, *Roman*, 9.

9. Peter Flax, "Roman Polanski Is Far from Silent."

10. Charlie Rose, "Roman Polanski," *Charlie Rose*, March 9, 2000, reprinted in Cronin, *Roman Polanski: Interviews*, 179.

11. Bernard Weinraub, "'If You Don't Show Violence the Way It Is . . .'"

12. Polanski, *Roman*, 97.

13. Ibid., 94.

14. Piotr Kaminski, "I Was Part of the Welles Group," *L'Avant-Scène Cinema*, December 1983; reprinted in Cronin, *Roman Polanski: Interviews*, 98–99.

15. Bird, "My Brilliant Career."

16. DuBois, "Playboy Interview: Roman Polanski," 96.

17. Bird, "My Brilliant Career."

18. Jerzy Skolimowski, Interview on *Knife in the Water* DVD (The Criterion Collection, 2002).

19. Gelmis, "Roman Polanski," *The Film Director as Superstar*, 146.

20. Thompson, "The Road to *Repulsion*."

21. Masterman, "Through the Mirror of Surrealism."

22. Tom Burke, "The Restoration of Roman Polanski," *Rolling Stone*, July 18, 1974.

23. Philippe Haudiquet, *Les lettres françaises*, January 13, 1966, reprinted in Cronin, *Roman Polanski: Interviews*, 9.

SETTING THE WHEELS IN MOTION

1. DuBois, "Playboy Interview," 100.

2. Polanski, *Roman*, 185.

3. Reisner and Kane, "An Interview with Roman Polanski," 11.

4. DuBois, "Playboy Interview," 118.

5. Reisner and Kane, "Interview," 12.

6. Robert Laffont, ed., "My Best Film: *Cul-de-Sac*," *L'Avant-Scene Cinema*, no. 571, Apr. 2008.

7. Ibid.

8. Polanski, *Roman*, 190.

9. Butler, *The Cinema of Roman Polanski*, 91.

10. Polanski, *Roman*, 190.

11. Reisner and Kane, "Interview," 12.

12. Polanski, *Roman*, 191.

13. "Dutch Production Guide," *Variety*, May 8, 1963.

14. Polanski, *Roman*, 202.

15. *Variety*, September 18, 1963.

16. Gutowski, *With Balls and Chutzpah*, 199.

17. Constantin Nsar, "Dance Macabre," *Little Shoppe of Horrors*, 66.

18. *Polanski: A Film Memoir*.

19. "In the Picture," *The Observer* (London), March 29, 1964.

20. Tom Vallance, "Tony Tenser," *Independent* (UK), December 19, 2007.

21. Spicer and McKenna, *The Man Who Got Carter*, 33.

22. Hamilton, *Beasts in the Cellar*, 37.

23. Paul Rowlands, "Tony Klinger on Michael Klinger." *Money Into Light,* January 16, 2012. http://www.money-into-light.com/2012/01/man-who -got-carter-and-polanski-caine.html

24. Tony Klinger, email to the author, November 8, 2021.

25. Tony Klinger, email to the author, October 17, 2016.

26. Ibid.

27. Rowlands, "Michael Klinger."

28. Polanski, *Roman*, 208.

29. Bird, "My Brilliant Career."

30. Gutowski, *With Balls and Chutzpah*, 200.

31. Hamilton, *Beasts in the Cellar*, 38.

32. Gutowski, *With Balls and Chutzpah*, 222.

33. Klinger, email to the author, November 8, 2021.

34. Compton posters and lobby cards, accessed online, August 16, 2016.

35. Roger Simons, interview with the author from London via Skype, June 14, 2016.

36. Tony Klinger, email to the author, October 17, 2016.

37. Gutowski, *With Balls and Chutzpah*, 221.

38. Polanski, *Roman*, 209.

39. *Polanski: A Film Memoir.*

40. Bird, "My Brilliant Career."

41. Polanski, *Roman*, 223.

WHEELING AND DEALING

1. Berlinale website, https://www.berlinale.de/en/archive/jahresarchive /1965/01_jahresblatt_1965/01_jahresblatt_1965.html

2. "German Govt. Awards 3 Pix," *Weekly Variety*, February 10, 1965.

3. Alexander Walker, "This Grim, Grim Picture the Censor Passed Uncut!" *Evening Standard* (London), May 20, 1965, p. 12.

4. Klinger, email to the author, October 21, 2016.

5. *Variety*, June 2, 1965.

6. Klinger, email to the author, October 20, 2016.

7. Ibid.

8. Hamilton, *Beasts in the Cellar*, 65.

9. Ibid, 75.

10. Klinger, email to the author, October 17, 2016.

11. Reisner and Kane, "Interview," 12.

12. Gutowski, interview with the author, London, June 12, 1975.

13. Franz-Olivier Giesbert, "Roman's Novel," *Le Nouvel Observateur*, April 13, 1984; reprinted in Cronin, *Roman Polanski: Interviews*.

14. Simons, interview with the author.

15. Fionnuala Kenny, email to the author, November 16, 2016.

16. Simons, interview with the author.

17. Klinger, email, October 20, 2016.

18. Robin O'Donoghue, interview with the author, from London via Zoom, March 17, 2021.

19. Tony Tenser, *Two Gangsters and an Island*.

20. Ibid.

21. Hamilton, *Beasts in the Cellar*, 77.

22. William Franklyn, *Two Gangsters and an Island*.

23. McKenna and Spicer, "Interview with Gerry Arbeid," October 12, 2010, http://michaelklingerpapers.uwe.ac.uk/arbeid.htm

24. Greenberg, *A Retrospective*, 69.

25. "Berlin Unter den Festival," *Weekly Variety*, July 7, 1965.

26. *Weekly Variety*, July 14, 1965.

27. Hamilton, *Beasts in the Cellar*, 77.

28. Klinger, email to the author, October 17, 2016.

29. O'Donoghue, interview with the author.

30. Simons, interview with the author.

31. Movement Order, June 3, 1965, courtesy of Simons.

32. Simons, interview with the author.

33. Polanski, *Roman*, 241.

34. Ibid., 238.

35. Gutowski, *With Balls and Chutzpah*, 238.

36. Weinraub, "'If You Don't Show Violence the Way It Is . . .'"

37. Greenberg, *A Retrospective*, 152.

CASTING THE NET

1. Bird, "My Brilliant Career."

2. Polanski and Brach, *Katelbach*, 6.

3. Klinger, email to the author, October 24, 2016.

4. Ross and Ross, "Donald Pleasence," 267.

5. Ibid., 259.

6. Irving Drutman, "Pleasence Without Makeup," *New York Times*, November 22, 1964, X5.

7. Ross and Ross, "Donald Pleasence," 262.

8. "Donald Pleasence," *Current Biography*.

9. Ross and Ross, "Donald Pleasence," 263.

10. Ibid., 264.

11. Ibid.

12. Gullo, *The Films of Donald Pleasence*, 59.

13. Bosley Crowther, "Screen: Unruly and Irritating Visitor," *New York Times*, January 21, 1964.

14. Mary Blume, "Donald Pleasence—Proud of His Wicked Film Ways," *Los Angeles Times*, July 21, 1968.

15. Drutman, "Pleasence Without Makeup."

16. Polanski, *Roman*, 163.

17. Butler, *Cinema*, 108.

18. Polanski, *Two Gangsters and an Island*.

19. Polanski and Brach, *Katelbach*, 1.

20. Polanski, *Roman*, 164.

21. Ibid., 224.

22. Ibid.

23. Lawrenson, "Who Is the World's Foremost Actor? . . . " *Esquire*, December 1, 1967.

24. Guy Flatley, "Lionel Stander: Who's Afraid of John Wayne?" *New York Times*, May 23, 1971.

25. Lawrenson, "Who Is the World's Foremost Actor?"

26. "S.S. Glencairn," *New York Times*, January 10, 1929.

27. Bob Weiskopf, interview with the author, Los Angeles, February 4, 1992.

28. McGilligan and Buhle, "Lionel Stander."

29. Lawrenson, "Who Is the World's Foremost Actor?"

30. McGilligan and Buhle, "Lionel Stander."

31. "Says Reds Sought Hollywood Cash," *New York Times*, August 7, 1940.

32. "No Deal," *New York Times*, January 12, 1947.

33. "Being a Red Called Hideous Mistake," *New York Times*, April 25, 1951.

34. Peter Kihss, "Stander Lectures House Red Inquiry," *New York Times*, May 7, 1953; Eric Bentley, ed. *Excerpts from Hearings Before the House Committee on Un-American Activities, 1938–1968* (New York: Viking Press, 1971).

35. McGilligan and Buhle, "Lionel Stander."

36. Howard Taubman, "Theater: Bertolt Brecht's 'Arturo Ui,'" *New York Times*, November 12, 1963.

37. Lawrenson, "Who Is the World's Foremost Actor?"

38. Polanski and Brach, *Katelbach*, 1.

39. Polanski, "Tribute to Jack MacGowran," program note, London, June 1973.

40. Roman Polanski, interview with the author, Los Angeles, May 9, 1974.

41. Gloria MacGowran, interview with the author, London, June 22, 1975.

42. Hilton Edwards, interview with the author, Dublin, July 10, 1975.

43. Jack MacGowran, interview with the author, Los Angeles, February 13, 1972.

44. Gloria MacGowran, interview with the author.

45. Ibid.

46. Richard Toscan, "MacGowran on Beckett," *Theatre Quarterly*, July–September 1973.

47. Kenneth Tynan, *Curtains* (New York: Atheneum, 1961).

48. Ruby Cohn, *Just Play: Beckett's Theatre* (Princeton NJ: Princeton University Press, 1980).

49. *Irish Times*, October 30, 1959.

50. Peter O'Toole, interview with the author, London, September 26, 1975.

51. Gloria MacGowran, interview with the author.

52. Critic unknown, cited by Gabriel Fallon, *Evening Press*, July 25, 1964.

53. *Endgame* program note reported by Fallon, *Evening Press*, 1969.

54. Derek Malcolm, "The Day the Malt Fused," *Guardian*, December 30, 1964.

55. Polanski and Brach, *Katelbach*, 3.

56. Polanski, *Two Gangsters and an Island*.

57. Parker, *Polanski*, 92.

58. Ibid., 93.

59. Ibid.

60. Pleasence, interview with the author, Los Angeles, March 19, 1977.

61. Polanski, *Roman*, 225.

62. *Hello! Magazine*, #248, April 10, 1993.

63. Roderick Mann, "Bisset on Nudity," *Los Angeles Times*, May 14, 1978.

64. Polanski, *Roman*, 225.

65. Stewart, *Mon bel âge*, ebook, location 1243/1248.

66. Polanski, *Roman*, 225.

67. Stewart, *Mon bel âge*, location 1248.

68. Ibid., location 2172.

69. Pleasence, interview with the author.

70. Deneuve and Modiano, *Elle s'appelait Françoise*.

71. Ibid.

72. "Soft Skin: The Brief and Intense Life of Françoise Dorléac," *Le Monde*, July 3, 1988.

73. Ibid.

74. Dorléac quoted in photo caption, *Indianapolis Star*, January 10, 1966.

75. Deneuve and Modiano, *Elle s'appelait Françoise*.

76. Suzanne Lowry, "Why I Could Never Share My Grief for My Sister until Now," *Evening Standard* (London), November 22, 1996.

77. George T. Harris, "Sister Stars of France," *Look*, June 1, 1965.

78. Deneuve and Modiano, *Elle s'appelait Françoise*.

79. Melissa Anderson, "Almost Famous," *Film Comment*, July–August 2005.

80. Deneuve and Modiano, *Elle s'appelait Françoise*.

81. Patrick Thévenon, "Interview with Catherine Deneuve and Françoise Dorléac," *L'Express*, 1966.

82. Polanski, *Roman*, 225.

83. Klinger, email to the author, October 25, 2016.

84. Polanski, *Roman*, 213.

85. Gutowski, *Two Gangsters and an Island*.

86. Polanski and Brach, *Katelbach*, 80.

87. Shearer, "Sharon Tate."

88. Statman and Tate, *Restless Souls*.

89. Polanski, *Roman*, 250.

90. Tate cited in "New Sex Goddess—Handle with Love," *Movie TV Secrets*, October 1967, reprinted in *Little Shoppe of Horrors*, 76.

RECRUITING THE CREW

1. Kenny, email to the author, November 7, 2016.

2. Joe Roman, email to the author, September 13, 2016.

3. Simon Farquar, "Voytek," *Independent* (UK), November 4, 2014.

4. Ibid.

5. *A Film Memoir*.

6. Polanski, *Roman*, 210.

7. Williams, "High Key Highlights."

8. James Hughes, "A Long Time Ago . . . ," *Slate*, August 23, 2013.

9. Paul Young, "Taylor Made," *Daily Variety*, February 24, 2006.

10. "Gilbert Taylor, Star Wars cinematographer, dies aged 99," BBC, August 23, 2013, https://www.bbc.com/news/entertainment-arts-23808854

11. Ibid.

12. Williams, "High Key Highlights."

13. Taylor, *Two Gangsters and an Island*.

14. Ibid.

15. Reed, "Roman Polanski."

16. O'Donoghue, interview with the author.

17. Cezary Lerski, comp. "Krzysztof Komeda: Bio." https://www.polish jazz.com/komeda.

18. Polanski, *Roman*, 148.

19. Parker, *Polanski*, 100.

20. Nasr, "Dance Macabre," 70.

21. Reisner and Kane, "Interview," 14.

22. Hendrykowski, email to the author, May 15, 2017.

23. Polanski, *Roman*, 211.

24. Simons, interview with the author.

25. O'Donoghue, interview with the author.

26. Polanski, *Roman*, 220.

27. Peter Musgrave, "Stephen Dalby: Obituary," *The Journal*, no. 67, June 2011.

28. O'Donoghue, interview with the author.

29. Ibid.

30. Simons, interview with the author.

31. Polanski, *Roman*, 214.

32. Simons, interview with the author.

33. Ibid.

34. Polanski, *Two Gangsters and an Island*.

35. Simons, interview with the author.

FROM SCRIPT TO SCREEN

1. Polanski, *Two Gangsters and an Island*.
2. Gelmis, "Roman Polanski," 147.
3. Kenny, email to the author, November 8, 2016.
4. Polanski and Brach, *Katelbach*, 31.
5. Polanski and Brach, *Katelbach*, 13.
6. Anthony Balducci, "The Incredible Laughable Egg," July 2016, available at: http://anthonybalducci.blogspot.com/search/?q=The+Incredible +Laughable+Egg
7. Polanski, *Roman*, 164.
8. Butler, *Cinema*, 109.
9. Ibid.
10. Stander, interview with the author via phone from Los Angeles, June 6, 1976.
11. Polanski and Brach, *Katelbach*, 69.
12. Polanski and Brach, *Katelbach*, 74.
13. Pleasence, interview with the author.
14. Gutowski, interview with the author.
15. MacGowran, interview with the author.
16. Polanski, interview with the author.
17. MacGowran, interview with the author.
18. Polanski and Brach, *Katelbach*, 50.
19. Ibid., 24.
20. Ibid., 94.
21. Trevor Delaney, email to the author, June 2, 2022.
22. Polanski and Brach, *Katelbach*, 97.
23. Ibid., 106.
24. Ibid., 111.
25. Ibid., 118–19.
26. Ibid., 119.
27. Klinger, email to the author, October 25, 2016.
28. Sandford, *Polanski*, 89.
29. Greenberg, *A Retrospective*, 62.

30. Thomson, "High Tides."

31. James Knowlson, *Damned to Fame: The Life of Samuel Beckett* (New York: Simon & Schuster, 1996), 343.

32. Polanski and Brach, *Katelbach*, 17.

33. Ibid., 110.

34. "View from Local Vantage Point," *New York Times*, October 27, 1963.

35. Irving Wardle, "Comedy of Menace," *Encore* 5, September–October 1958, pp. 28–33.

36. Michel Ciment, et al., "Interview with Roman Polanski," *Positif,* February 1969; reprinted in Cronin, *Roman Polanski: Interviews.*

37. Gelmis, "Roman Polanski," 150.

38. Thomson, "High Tides."

39. Coates, "*Cul-de-Sac* in Context."

40. French, *Observer* (London), June 5, 1966.

41. Polanski, interview with the author.

42. Beckett, letter to MacGowran, December 13, 1967, Harry Ransom Humanities Resource Center, University of Texas, Austin.

BEHIND THE SCENES

1. Polanski and Brach, *Katelbach*, 1, 3.

2. Gutowski, *With Balls and Chutzpah*, 236.

3. Ibid.

4. Polanski, *Two Gangsters and an Island.*

5. Polanski, *Roman*, 223.

6. Voytek, *Two Gangsters and an Island.*

7. Polanski, *Two Gangsters and an Island.*

8. Fionnuala Kenny, email to the author, November 8, 2016.

9. Franklyn, *Two Gangsters and an Island.*

10. Voytek, *Two Gangsters and an Island.*

11. Call sheet, June 18, 1965, courtesy of Polanski.

12. Gutowski, *With Balls and Chutzpah*, 237.

13. Ibid., 238.

14. O'Donoghue, interview with the author.

15. Polanski, *Two Gangsters and an Island*.

16. Polanski, *Roman*, 226.

17. Ibid.

18. Pleasence, interview with the author.

19. Taylor, *Two Gangsters and an Island*.

20. Gutowski, interview with the author.

21. Simons, interview with the author.

22. Polanski *Roman*, 228.

23. Will Jones, "after last night," *Star Tribune* (Minneapolis), May 6, 1972, p. 12A.

24. Gutowski, interview with the author.

25. Leaming, *Polanski*, 72.

26. Angela Pleasence, email to the author, November 2, 2016.

27. Gutowski, *With Balls and Chutzpah*, 236.

28. O'Donoghue, interview with the author.

29. Gutowski, *Two Gangsters and an Island*.

30. Polanski, *Roman*, 226.

31. Gutowski, interview with the author.

32. Jones, "after last night."

33. Taylor, *Two Gangsters and an Island*.

34. Simons, interview with the author.

35. Nick Lewis, email to the author, March 26, 2021.

36. Simons, interview with the author.

37. Polanski, *Roman*, 228.

38. Pleasence, interview with the author.

39. Jones, "after last night."

40. Polanski, *Roman*, 228.

41. Thompson, "The Road to *Repulsion*."

42. Stander, interview with the author.

43. Polanski, *Roman*, 228.

44. Sandford, *Polanski*.

45. Polanski, *Roman*, 226.

46. Melissa Parker, "Jacqueline Bisset Interview," *Smashing Interviews*, November 19, 2015.

47. Simons, interview with the author.

48. Klinger, email to the author, October 24, 2016.

49. Simons, interview with the author.

50. Ibid.

51. Polanski, *Roman*, 238.

52. Simons, interview with the author.

53. Ibid.

54. Polanski, *Roman*, 227.

55. Simons, interview with the author.

56. O'Donoghue, interview with the author.

57. Kenny, email to the author, November 16, 2016.

58. Delaney, email to the author.

59. Polanski, *Roman*, 217.

60. Simons, interview with the author.

61. O'Donoghue, interview with the author.

62. Ibid.

63. Ibid.

64. Sandford, *Polanski*.

65. Simons, interview with the author.

66. O'Donoghue, interview with the author.

67. Gutowski, *Two Gangsters and an Island*.

68. Butler, *Cinema*, 114.

69. Polanski, *Two Gangsters and an Island*.

70. Butler, *Cinema*, 189.

71. Weinraub, "If You Don't Show Violence the Way It Is."

72. O'Donoghue, interview with the author.

73. *Komeda Komeda*.

74. Polanski, *Roman*, 245.

THE TROUBLE WITH ACTORS

1. Philippe Haudiquet, *Les lettres françaises*, January 13, 1966, reprinted in Cronin, *Roman Polanski: Interviews*, 11.

2. Polanski, *Roman*, 227.

3. Gelmis, "Roman Polanski," 147.

4. Simons, interview with the author.

5. Weinraub, " 'If You Don't Show Violence the Way It Is'"

6. Polanski, *Roman*, 217.

7. Polanski, *Two Gangsters and an Island.*

8. Lewis, "Mad Dogs and an Englishman."

9. Butler, *Cinema*, 108.

10. Stander, interview with the author.

11. Simons, interview with the author.

12. Stander, interview with the author.

13. Simons, interview with the author.

14. Sandford, *Polanski*, 91.

15. Butler, *Cinema*, 109.

16. Angela Pleasence, email to the author.

17. Simons, interview with the author.

18. Polanski, *Roman*, 237.

19. Stander, interview with the author.

20. Leaming, *Polanski*, 72.

21. Bella Stander, email to the author, November 4, 2016.

22. Polanski, *Roman*, 237.

23. Lionel Stander, interview with James L. Neibaur via phone, circa 1986.

24. Polanski, *Two Gangsters and an Island.*

25. Ibid.

26. Bella Stander, interview with the author via phone from New York, November 16, 2016.

27. Polanski, *Two Gangsters and an Island.*

28. Ibid.

29. Simons, interview with the author.

30. Bella Stander, interview with the author.

31. Simons, interview with the author.

32. O'Donoghue, email to the author, April 7, 2022.

33. Polanski, *Roman*, 215.

34. Leaming, *Polanski*, 69–70.

35. Butler, *Cinema*, 110.

36. Miller, "An Actress Alone."

37. Simons, interview with the author.

38. Polanski, *Roman*, 238.

39. David Del Valle, "Interview with the Vampire," *Little Shoppe of Horrors*, 84.

40. Taylor, *Two Gangsters and an Island.*

41. Polanski, interview with the author.

42. Butler, *Cinema*, 182.

43. Nsar, "The Professor's Daughter Speaks," *Little Shoppe of Horrors*, 46.

44. Polanski, *Roman*, 226.

45. Polanski, interview with the author.

46. Gutowski, interview with the author.

47. Simons, interview with the author.

48. Polanski, interview with the author.

A DAY AT THE BEACH

1. Polanski, *Two Gangsters and an Island.*

2. Polanski, *Roman*, 240.

3. Bill Dial, "2 Great Films . . . ," *Atlanta Constitution*, Atlanta, January 4, 1968.

4. O'Donoghue, interview with the author.

5. Associated Press, "Nudity for Art's Sake Is OK, Not Sensationalism," *Sacramento Bee*, August 10, 1966.

6. Polanski, *Roman*, 240.

7. Jones, "after last night."

8. Polanski, *Roman*, 240.

9. Butler, *Cinema*, 114.

10. O'Donoghue, interview with the author.

11. Simons, interview with the author.

12. Gutowski, *Two Gangsters and an Island.*

13. Leaming, *Polanski*, 70–71.

14. Polanski, *Roman*, 240.

15. Simons, interview with the author.
16. Polanski, *Roman*, 240.
17. Miller, "An Actress Alone."
18. Polanski, *Roman*, 240.
19. Taylor, *Two Gangsters and an Island.*
20. O'Donoghue, interview with the author.
21. Simons, interview with the author.
22. Delaney, email to the author.
23. Sterritt, "*Cul-de-Sac.*"
24. O'Donoghue, interview with the author.
25. Gutowski, *Two Gangsters and an Island.*
26. François Truffaut, *Hitchcock* (New York: Touchstone, 1967), 131.

RELEASE AND CRITICAL RECEPTION

1. British Film Institute, "10 Great Films from 1966," www2.bfi.org.uk.
2. Ibid.
3. Dominic Maillet, *Cinematographe*, Mar. 1981; reprinted in Cronin, *Roman Polanski: Interviews*, 88.
4. Michel Delahaye & Jean Narboni, *Cahiers du Cinema*, Jan. 1969; reprinted in Cronin, *Roman Polanski: Interviews*, 21.
5. Hamilton, *Beasts in the Cellar,* 78.
6. Ibid, 65.
7. *Times*, June 2, 1966.
8. Vincent Canby, "X-Rated Polanski," *New York Times*, October 4, 1973.
9. "The Story of *Cul-de-Sac*," Compton-Cameo press release, 1966.
10. Richard Roud, *Guardian*, June 3, 1966.
11. Dilys Powell, *Sunday Times,* June 5, 1966.
12. Isabel Quigley, *Spectator*, June 3, 1966.
13. D. W., *Monthly Film Bulletin*, BFI, July 1966.
14. Alexander Walker, *Evening Standard* (London), June 2, 1966.
15. "Berlin Film Prize to British Entry," *New York Times*, July 6, 1966.
16. *Weekly Variety*, July 13, 1966.

17. Harold Myers, "Buyers Too Few, Prizes Too Contrived at Berlin," *Weekly Variety*, July 13, 1966.

18. Hollis Alpert, *Saturday Review*, December 10, 1966.

19. Myers, "Buyers Too Few, Prizes Too Contrived at Berlin."

20. Rowlands, "Michael Klinger."

21. "International Sound Track," *Weekly Variety*, June 22, 1966.

22. *Cul-de-Sac*, Italian poster.

23. Pierre Marcabru, *Arts*; reprinted in *L'Avant-Scène Cinema*, no. 571 (April 2008).

24. Pierre Billard, *L'Express*; reprinted in *L'Avant-Scène Cinema*.

25. Jean Collet, *Télérama*; reprinted in *L'Avant-Scène Cinema*.

26. John Trevelyan, BBFC, letter to Polanski, February 8, 1966; reprinted in Philip Nutman, "Dancing with Vampires," *Little Shoppe of Horrors*, 36.

27. Polanski, *Roman*, 250.

28. Reed, "Roman Polanski," 12.

29. Gelmis, "Roman Polanski," 153.

30. *New York Daily News*, November 8, 1966.

31. Crowther, "'Repulsion'—the 'Psycho' of '65," *New York Times*, October 4, 1965.

32. Crowther, "The Screen: Polanski's Wild Swing," *New York Times*, November 8, 1966.

33. Gelmis, "*Cul-de-Sac* Is Fun, Horror That Winds Up as a Dead End," *Newsday*, November 8, 1966.

34. Sarris, *Village Voice*, December 1, 1966.

35. Gill, "Dead End," *New Yorker*, November 12, 1966.

36. Crowther, *New York Times*, August 14, 1967.

37. Crowther, "They Bite, But Can They Chew?" *New York Times*, November 20, 1966.

38. Crowther, "The Screen: Polanski's Wild Swing."

39. Dennis McLellan, "Judith Crist Dies at 90," *Los Angeles Times*, August 8, 2012.

40. Crist, *New York World Journal Tribune*, November 20, 1966.

41. US pressbook, Filmways-Sigma III, 1966.

42. *Chicago Tribune*, January 1, 1968.

43. Reisner and Kane, "Interview," 12.

44. Alpert, *Saturday Review*, December 10, 1966.

45. *Variety*, November 16, 1966.

46. Ebert, *Chicago Sun-Times*, December 28, 1967.

47. Thomas, *Los Angeles Times*, January 17, 1968.

48. Glenn Erickson, "The Fearless Vampire Killers: A Tale of Two Versions," *DVD Savant*, December 8, 1999.

49. Erickson, Facebook message to the author, December 1, 2021.

50. Patrick Gibbs, *Daily Telegraph*, June 3, 1966.

51. *Variety*, June 3, 1966.

52. Hibbin, *Morning Star*, June 4, 1966.

53. Thomas, *Los Angeles Times*.

54. *Daily Mail*, June 4, 1966.

55. Les Wedman, "Les Wedman," *Vancouver Sun*, May 15, 1968.

56. *Monthly Film Bulletin*.

57. Ebert, *Chicago Sun-Times*.

58. Crowther, *New York Times*.

59. Gullo, *The Films of Donald Pleasence*, 18.

60. *Montreal Gazette*, August 16, 1968.

61. Robinson, *Sunday Telegraph*.

62. Wedman, "Les Wedman."

63. Ebert, *Chicago Sun-Times*.

64. *Time*, November 18, 1966.

65. Terry, "'Blind Alley' Is a Dead End," *Chicago Tribune*.

66. Gill, "Dead End."

67. Ann Pacey, *Sun*, June 2, 1966.

68. Michel Aubriant, *Paris Presse*; reprinted in *L'Avant-Scène Cinema*.

69. Rich, *Variety*, June 8, 1966.

70. Gibbs, The *Daily Telegraph*.

71. Leo Sullivan, *Washington Post*, February 18, 1967.

REVIVAL AND REASSESSMENT

1. Peary, "1966: The Best Choice: *Cul-de-Sac*," 182–83.

2. *Schenectady Gazette*, July 18, 1968.

3. Dane Lanken, *Montreal Gazette*, August 16, 1968.

4. Wedman, "Les Wedman."

5. Raymond Durgnat, "Britannia Rules the Waves," *Film Comment*, July/August 1976, 50.

6. Nutman, *Little Shoppe of Horrors*, 53.

7. Kevin Thomas, *Los Angeles Times*, April 1, 1977.

8. British Board of Film Classification.

9. Priscilla Eyles, "*Cul-De-Sac*, Dir. Roman Polanski," February 1, 2009, https://priscillaeyles.wordpress.com/2009/02/01/cul-de-sac-dir-roman-polanski-1966/#more-7.

10. Kevin Hagopian, SUNY program, 2004, www.albany.edu/writers-inst.

11. Karen Stetler, email to the author, February 15, 2017.

12. Ron Deutsch, "TV Bites: *Cul-de-Sac*," *Chef du Cinema*, August 27, 2011, http://chef-du-cinema.blogspot.com/2011/08/tv-bites-cul-de-sac.html.

13. Wilmington, "Pick of the Week: Classic."

14. Nathaniel Thompson, *Mondo Digital*, August 9, 2011.

15. Morgan, "*Cul-de-Sac*."

16. Sterritt, "*Cul-de-Sac*."

17. Josh Rottenberg, "What'll Become of the Cult Movie?," *Los Angeles Times*, October 30, 2016, 1.

18. Bella Stander, Facebook post, November 4, 2016.

19. Stander, interview with the author.

20. Simon Columb, *Flickering Myth*, flickeringmyth.com, January 15, 2013.

21. Greenberg, *A Retrospective*, 138.

22. Mazierska, *Roman Polanski*, 69.

23. Coates, "*Cul-de-Sac* in Context."

24. Eugene Ionesco, *Rhinoceros and Other Plays* (New York: Grove Press, 1960).

25. Glenn Erickson, "Roman Polanski's *Cul-de-Sac* on DVD," *TCM*, August 2011, http://www.tcm.com.

26. Jan Herman, *A Talent for Trouble* (New York: G. P. Putnam's Sons, 1995).

27. Mazierska, *Roman Polanski*, 169.

28. Fernando F. Croce, *CinePassion*, November 18, 2013, http://www.cinepassion.org/Reviews/c/CuldeSac.html.

29. Michel Ciment and Hubert Niogret, "Interview with Joel and Ethan Coen: In Regard to *Barton Fink*," *Positif*, September 1991.

30. Andy Klein, "Polanski's Babies," *Los Angeles Reader*, March 11, 1994, 21.

31. Alexander Walker, "Madhouse on the Road to the Isles," *Evening Standard* (London), May 8, 2003, 44.

32. Owen Gleiberman, *Entertainment Weekly*, March 12, 2008.

33. spaceodds, December 22, 2013, 9:49 p.m., comment on "In Bruges (2008)–A Review," http://haphazardstuffblog.com/in-bruges-2008-a-review/

34. Paul Rooney, "Still at Large," http://www.paulrooney.info/new-theme-to-still-at-large/.

THE WRAP PARTY

1. "Evil Head of SPECTRE Unmasked in Latest Film," *Edmonton Journal*, December 31, 1966.

2. *Stage & Cinema*, Johannesburg, November 12, 1965.

3. Thomas Quinn Curtiss, "Robert Shaw Play Staged in London," *New York Times*, July 29, 1967.

4. Pleasence, interview with the author.

5. Gullo, *The Films of Donald Pleasence*, 210.

6. Ibid., 32.

7. Anthony Hayward, "Obituaries: Donald Pleasence," *Independent* (UK), February 3, 1995.

8. Pleasence, interview with the author.

9. Hayward, "Donald Pleasence."

10. Gullo, *The Films of Donald Pleasence*, 36

11. Deneuve and Modiano, *Elle s'appelait Françoise*.

12. Miller, "An Actress Alone."

13. "Françoise Dorléac," obituary, *Los Angeles Times*, June 28, 1967.

14. Deneuve and Modiano, *Elle s'appelait Françoise.*

15. Miller, "An Actress Alone."

16. Deneuve and Modiano, *Elle s'appelait Françoise.*

17. *Newsweek*, July 20, 1967.

18. Associated Press, "Nudity for Art's Sake Is OK, Not Sensational-ism," *Sacramento Bee*, August 10, 1966.

19. Deneuve and Modiano, *Elle s'appelait Françoise.*

20. Thévenon, "Interview with Catherine Deneuve and Françoise Dorléac."

21. Deneuve and Modiano, *Elle s'appelait Françoise.*

22. François Truffaut, "Elle s'appelait Françoise," *Cahiers du cinéma*, April–May 1968.

23. Lawrenson, "Who Is the World's Foremost Actor?"

24. Bella Stander, interview with the author.

25. Allen Garfield, "Despite Talent, Kazan Doesn't Deserve Honorary Oscar," *Los Angeles Times*, January 25, 1999.

26. Robert J. Wagner with Scott Eyman, *Pieces of My Heart: A Life* (New York: Dey Street Books, 2008).

27. Seamus Kelly, *Irish Times*, August 3, 1966.

28. Lewis Funke, "MacGowran the Great," *New York Times*, December 6, 1970.

29. John Uterecker and Kathleen McGrory, eds., *Yeats, Joyce and Beckett* (Cranbury NJ: Associated University Press, 1976).

30. Toscan, "MacGowran on Beckett."

31. MacGowran, interview with the author.

32. Gloria MacGowran, interview with the author.

33. Mel Gussow, "The Quintessence of Beckett," *New York Times*, November 20, 1970.

34. Funke, "MacGowran the Great."

35. Polanski, interview with the author.

36. O'Toole, interview with the author.

37. Chollet, "The Man Who Wouldn't Go Out."

38. Françoise Audé et al., "Interview with Gérard Brach," *Positif*, no. 287, Jan. 1985, reprinted in Cronin, *Roman Polanski: Interviews*, 129.

39. Michel Ciment and Michel Sineux, "Interview with Roman Polanski," *Positif*, May 1988.

40. Chollet, "The Man Who Wouldn't Go Out."

41. Reed, "Roman Polanski."

42. Ibid.

43. Kevin Hilton, "Shadows Make Good Movies," *British Cinematographer*, November 2011, https://britishcinematographer.co.uk/all-time -greats-gilbert-taylor-bsc/

44. Paul Young, "Taylor Made."

45. Ibid.

46. Gutowski, *With Balls and Chutzpah*, 199.

47. Ibid.

48. Ibid., 2.

49. *Komeda Komeda*.

50. Lerski, "Krzysztof Komeda."

51. Ibid.

52. Leaming, *Polanski*, 63.

EPILOGUE

1. Butler, *Cinema*, 142.

2. William Castle, *Step Right Up!* (Los Angeles: William Castle Productions, 2010).

3. Robert Evans, *Remembering Rosemary's Baby*, on *Rosemary's Baby* DVD (The Criterion Collection, 2012).

4. "Most Distasteful Picture of '68: *Rosemary's Baby*," *Schenectady Gazette*, July 18, 1968.

5. Charles Higham, "Polanski: *Rosemary's Baby* and After," *New York Times*, September 23, 1973.

6. DuBois, "Playboy Interview," 98.

7. Ibid., 96–98.

8. Tuska, "Roman Polanski," 398.

9. Ibid., 375.

10. Jack Nicholson, interview with the author, Los Angeles, August 29, 1974.

11. "Clive James Meets Roman Polanski."

12. Samantha Geimer, *Larry King Live*, CNN, October 7, 2010, https://transcripts.cnn.com/show/lkl/date/2010-10-07/segment/01

13. Charles Champlin, "Polanski: Of Tess and Other Things," *Los Angeles Times*, May 21, 1979.

14. Charles Champlin, "Tess: Far from the Madding Marquees," *Los Angeles Times*, September 5, 1980.

15. Mary Blume, "Polanski the Romantic Tackles 'Tess,'" *Los Angeles Times*, November 18, 1979.

16. David Gritten, "On Location in Exile," *Los Angeles Times*, December 15, 1991.

17. Peter Rainer, "*Death and the Maiden*," *Los Angeles Times*, December 23, 1994.

18 Caryn James, "Apolitical Fable in Thriller's Clothing," *New York Times*, December 23, 1994.

19. Nasr, "Dancing with the Master," *Little Shoppe of Horrors*, 56.

20. Polanski, Audio commentary on *The Ninth Gate*, DVD (Lionsgate, 2000).

21. Greenberg, *A Retrospective*, 205.

22. Bird, "My Brilliant Career."

23. Polanski, Director's Statement, https://europeanfilmawards.eu/en_EN/film/the-pianist.5727.

24. Octavi Marti, "Memories of the Ghetto," *El Pais Semanal*, December 1, 2001; reprinted in Cronin, *Roman Polanski: Interviews*, 195.

25. Polanski, *Story of Survival*, on *The Pianist* DVD (Universal Studios, 2003).

26. Ben Kingsley, *Twist by Polanski*, on *Oliver Twist* DVD (Sony Pictures Home Entertainment, 2005).

27. Greenberg, *A Retrospective*, 239.

28. John Peterson, "Roman Polanski's *Carnage* Is a Joyously Unpleasant Film," *Guardian*, January 27, 2012.

29. David Ng, "For *Venus in Fur* Author, Working with Roman Polanski Was 'Heaven,'" *Los Angeles Times*, June 28, 2014.

30. David Hudson, "Roman Polanski's *An Officer and a Spy*," *The Daily*, Criterion.com, September 13, 2019.

31. Ibid.

32. Andreas Wiseman, "Roman Polanski Opens Up," *Deadline*, August 29, 2019.

33. Ibid.

34. Scott Foundas, "Roman Polanski Talks His Life and Career, *Venus in Fur* and Retirement," *Variety*, April 9, 2014.

BIBLIOGRAPHY

Alion, Yves, ed. "*Cul-de-Sac*: Roman Polanski." *L'Avant-Scène Cinema*, no. 571 (April 2008).

Audé, Françoise, et al. "Interview with Gérard Brach." *Positif*, no. 287 (January 1985).

Bergan, Ronald. "Gilbert Taylor obituary." *Guardian*, August 25, 2013.

Bird, Daniel. "Roman Polanski: My Brilliant Career." *Independent*, April 2, 2004.

Butler, Ivan. *The Cinema of Roman Polanski*. New York: A. S. Barnes & Co., 1970.

Coates, Paul. "*Cul-de-Sac* in Context: Absurd Authorship and Sexuality." In John Orr and Elizbeta Ostrowska, *The Cinema of Roman Polanski: Dark Spaces of the World*, 92–104. London: Wallflower Press, 2006.

Chollet, Laurence B. "The Man Who Wouldn't Go Out." *Los Angeles Times*, December 18, 1994.

Cronin, Paul, ed. *Roman Polanski: Interviews*. Jackson: University of Mississippi Press, 2005.

Crowther, Bosley. "The Screen: Polanski's Wild Swing." *New York Times*, November 8, 1966.

Deneuve, Catherine, and Patrick Modiano. *Elle s'appelait Françoise*. Paris: Canal + Editions, 1996.

"Donald Pleasence." *Current Biography*, June 1969.

DuBois, Larry. "Playboy Interview: Roman Polanski." *Playboy*, December 1971.

Flatley, Guy. "Lionel Stander: Who's Afraid of John Wayne?" *New York Times*, May 23, 1971.

Flax, Peter. "Roman Polanski Is Far from Silent." *Hollywood Reporter*, December 25, 2015.

Foundas, Scott. "Roman Polanski Talks His Life and Career, 'Venus in Fur' and Retirement." *Variety*, April 9, 2014.

Funke, Lewis. "MacGowran the Great." *New York Times*, December 6, 1970.

Gelmis, Joseph. "Roman Polanski." In *The Film Director as Superstar*, 139–55. New York: Doubleday & Co., 1970.

Grant, Lee. "Roman Polanski and the Hounds of Hell." *Los Angeles Times*, Calendar, May 1, 1977.

Greenberg, James. *Roman Polanski: A Retrospective*. New York: Abrams, 2013.

Gullo, Christopher. *The Films of Donald Pleasence*. Albany, GA: BearManor Media, 2012.

Gutowski, Gene. *With Balls & Chutzpah: A Story of Survival*. Bloomington, Indiana: iUniverse, 2011.

Hamilton, John. *Beasts in the Cellar: The Exploitation Film Career of Tony Tenser*. London: FAB Press, 2005.

Hickey, Des, and Gus Smith. "MacGowran: Waiting for Beckett." In *A Paler Shade of Green*. London: Frewin, 1972.

Internet Movie Database.

Jones, Will. "after last night." *Star Tribune*, Minneapolis, May 5, 1972.

Klemensen, Richard, ed. "The Fearless Vampire Killers." *Little Shoppe of Horrors: The Journal of Classic British Horror Films*, no. 27 (October 2011).

Komeda Komeda. (2012). Directed by Natasza Ziółkowska-Kurczuk. *Rosemary's Baby* DVD. Los Angeles: The Criterion Collection, 2012.

Lawrenson, Helen. "Who Is the World's Foremost Actor? . . ." *Esquire*, December 1, 1967.

Leaming, Barbara. *Polanski: A Biography*. New York: Simon & Schuster, 1981.

Lerski, Cezary, comp. "Krzysztof Komeda: Bio." Accessed August 8, 2016. https://www.polishjazz.com/komeda.

Lewis, Fiona. "Mad Dogs and an Englishman." *Los Angeles Times*, February 9, 1975.

Malcolm, Derek. "The Day the Malt Fused." *Guardian*, December 30, 1964.

Masterman, Len. "*Cul-de-Sac:* Through the Mirror of Surrealism." *Screen*, 11, no. 6 (November 1970), 44–60.

Mazierska, Ewa. *Roman Polanski: The Cinema of a Cultural Traveller.* London: I. B. Tauris, 2007.

McGilligan, Patrick, and Paul Buhle. "Lionel Stander." In *Tender Comrades: A Backstory of the Hollywood Blacklist*, 607–25. New York: St. Martin's Press, 1997.

Miller, Edwin. "An Actress Alone." *Seventeen*, November 1966.

Morgan, Kim. "*Cul-de-Sac.*" *Sunset Gun*, August 24, 2012. http://sunset gun.typepad.com/sunsetgun/

Parker, John. *Polanski.* London: Victor Gollancz, 1993.

Peary, Danny. "1966: The Best Choice: *Cul-de-Sac.*" In *Alternate Oscars*, 182–83. New York: A Delta Book, 1993.

Polanski, Roman. *Roman.* New York: William Morrow & Co., 1984.

———. *Three Film Scripts.* New York: Harper & Row, 1975.

Polanski, Roman, and Gérard Brach. *Katelbach.* Compton-Tekli Film Productions (unpublished, courtesy of Roman Polanski; copies housed at British Film Institute, London, and Cinémathèque française, Paris).

Polanski: A Film Memoir. DVD. Directed by Laurent Bouzereau. London: Network, 2011.

Reed, Rochelle, ed. "Roman Polanski." *Dialogue on Film*, American Film Institute. vol. 3, no. 8. (August 1974).

Reisner, Joel, and Bruce Kane. "An Interview with Roman Polanski." *Cinema*, vol. 5, no. 2 (1969).

Rosemary's Baby. DVD. Los Angeles: The Criterion Collection, 2012.

Ross, Lillian, and Helen Ross. "Donald Pleasence." In *The Player: A Profile of an Art*, 256–67. New York: Simon & Schuster, 1962.

Rowlands, Paul. "Tony Klinger on Michael Klinger." *Money Into Light*, January 16, 2012. http://www.money-into-light.com/2012/01/man-who-got-carter-and-polanski-caine.html

Sanders, Andrew. "Voytek obituary." *The Guardian*, August 15, 2014.

Sandford, Christopher. *Polanski: A Biography*. London: Century, 2007.

Spicer, Andrew, and A. T. McKenna, *The Man Who Got Carter: Michael Klinger, Independent Production and the British Film Industry, 1960–1980*. London: I. B. Tauris, 2013.

Shearer, Lloyd. "Sharon Tate: Sweetie, I'm Going to Make You a Star." *Detroit Free Press*, September 18, 1966.

Stander, Bella. "Lionel Stander: A Hollywood Story." *Albemarle*, October–November 2002.

Statman, Alisa, with Brie Tate. *Restless Souls: The Sharon Tate Family's Account of Stardom, the Manson Murders, and a Crusade for Justice*. New York: Dey Street Books, 2012.

Sterritt, David. "*Cul-de-Sac*." *Cineaste*, vol. 37, no. 1 (Winter 2011).

Stewart, Alexandra. *Mon bel âge*. Paris: Éditions de l'Archipel, 2014. Kindle Edition.

Thompson, Howard. "The Road to *Repulsion*." *New York Times*, November 14, 1965.

Thomson, David. "High Tides." *Cul-de-Sac* DVD booklet. Los Angeles: The Criterion Collection, 2011.

Tuska, Jon, ed. "Roman Polanski." In *Close-Up: The Contemporary Director*, 369–409. Metuchen NJ: Scarecrow Press, 1981.

Two Gangsters and an Island. (2003). Directed by David Gregory. *Cul-de-Sac* DVD. Los Angeles: The Criterion Collection, 2011.

Wedman, Les. "Les Wedman." *Vancouver Sun*, May 15, 1968.

Weedman, Christopher. "The Man with the Hypnotic Eye." Accessed July 29, 2017. http://www.pleasence.com/BIO-DP.HTML.

Weinraub, Bernard. " 'If You Don't Show Violence the Way It Is,' Says Roman Polanski . . ." *New York Times*, December 12, 1971.

Williams, David E. "High Key Highlights." *American Cinematographer* 87, no. 2 (February 2006).

Wilmington, Mike. "Pick of the Week: Classic." *Movie City News*, August 31, 2011.

Young, Jordan R. *The Beckett Actor: Jack MacGowran, Beginning to End*. Beverly Hills: Moonstone Press, 1987.

INDEX

Note: Page numbers in *italics* reference photographs.

Papp, Joseph, 175
Parker, John, 47
The Passenger (film), 133
Peary, Danny, 153
Peckinpah, Sam, 162
Pegley, Alf, 71, 106
The Pianist (film), 156, 180, 189
Pinter, Harold, 30, 34, 88–90, *89*, 164, 167
Pirates (film), 27, 71, 178, 187
The Pixies, 164
Planet Films GmbH, 12–13
Playboy Enterprises, 27
The Player (film), 133
Pleasence, Angela, 100, 114, 117, 167
Pleasence, Donald
    background, 30–36, *31*, 58, 88, 89–90, *89*
    comparison to Kingsley, 160
    on *Cul-de-Sac* casting decisions, 47, 51, 89–90
    Cul-de-Sac casting of, 30, 35–36, 41
    Cul-de-Sac film schedule for, 26
    on *Cul-de-Sac* location, 98–99, 100, 102
    Cul-de-Sac on-set disagreements, 112–114, *115*, 119
    Cul-de-Sac performance reviews, 149–150, 151
    Cul-de-Sac retakes with, 108
    in *Cul-de-Sac* scene (deleted), *80*
    in *Cul-de-Sac* scene on beach, 125–127, *126*, 128, 129, *131*
    in *Cul-de-Sac* scenes (final), 84–85, *85*, 159
    in *Cul-de-Sac* scenes in bedroom, 78–79, *127*, 159–160
    Cul-de-Sac script improvisions by, 78
    death of, 167–168
    Pinter vibe of, 88
    post-*Cul-de-Sac* career, 166, 182
    at *Repulsion* premier, 20
    Voytek and, 63
Pleasence, Josephine, 113, 150
The Plough and the Stars (O'Casey), 45, 171, 175
Polanski, Roman. *See also specific films*
    affairs of, 104, 187, 190
    background, 1–4
    children of, 189–190
    marriages. *See* Kwiatkowska, Basia; Tate, Sharon
    perfectionism of, 6, 106–108, 109–110, 118, 122
    photos, *5*, *8*, *12*, *18*, *64*, *88*, *97*, *137*, *143*, *184–186*, *188*, *P-2*
    on reliving his life, 1
    sex-with-a-minor conviction, 187, 190
Polish Film Week, 13
Polonsky, Abraham, 180
Powell, Dilys, 139
Price, Vincent, 182
Private Property (film), 162
Pulp (film), 116, 182

Quarrier, Iain, 55, 120–121, *121*, 177
Quest for Fire (film), 178
Quest for Fire (Rosny), 178
The Quiet Man (film), *42*, 43, 44
Quigley, Isabel, 139
Quo Vadis (Sienkiewicz), 81

Rampling, Charlotte, 47
Ransohoff, Martin "Marty," 59, 136, 142–143, 148, 154
Ratliff, Ben, 181
Raymond, Miriam, 32

ABOUT THE AUTHOR

Jordan R. Young is the author of *Spike Jones Off the Record: The Man Who Murdered Music*; *The Beckett Actor: Jack MacGowran, Beginning to End*; *Acting Solo: The Art & Craft of Solo Performance*; *The Laugh Crafters: Comedy Writing in Radio and TV's Golden Age*; and *King Vidor's* The Crowd: *The Making of a Silent Classic*. His work has been published in the *New York Times, Los Angeles Times, Washington Post, Christian Science Monitor, Film International*, and *Millimeter*. His plays have been produced Off-Off-Broadway and in Hollywood. He has contributed to *Hal Ashby: Interviews*; *The Best Men's Monologues of 2021*; and *All Music Guide*. He has served as a writer or consultant for the Grammy Awards, BBC Radio, and Le Giornate del Muto Silent Film Festival in Pordenone, Italy.